OUR
COMPATIBLE
Grief

By
Deborah Anthony

Deborah Anthony

1672 Beaver Bank Road

Beaver Bank, Nova Scotia

CA   B4G 1C9

Copyright © 2025 Deborah Anthony

LCCN: 2025942221

Author Contact: Email: danthony@ns.sympatico.ca

Website: deborahanthony.com

All rights reserved. No part of this book may be reproduced, stored in a retrieval system, or transmitted in any form or by any means without the prior permission of the copyright holder, except for the purpose of short excerpts used in book reviews.

Anthony, Deborah 1951 -

Our Compatible Grief/Deborah Anthony

1. Children-Death   2. Bereavement   3. Self-help

IN HONOUR OF

Erin Margaret Anthony

June 3, 1978 – December 6, 1984

Erin Margaret Anthony was a little girl full of smiles who was fortunate enough to have enjoyed wisdom beyond her years and had a knack of bringing joy to all who crossed her path. She loved life, was spontaneous, and had been blessed with a very kind and generous spirit. She had a special affinity for animals and was always ready for an adventure in nature. Camping, bonfires and smores were favourites. Her beautiful profile is silhouetted on the cover of this book accompanied by her precious sister and best friend, Heather. Erin thought it was a wonderful picture of them both and she was right.

IN MEMORY OF

This book is dedicated in memory of all the children who have died and to remember their Moms and Dads who were not ready to let them go. Please honour your loved one by placing their name, photo, or anything else you may want to include about them below.

TABLE OF CONTENTS

Preface 1

Acknowledgements 3

Introduction 5

MASTERING THE ART OF JOURNALING

Prologue 8

Chapter 1 "The Journal" 10

Chapter 2 "The Mindset" 15

Chapter 3 "The Materials" 21

Chapter 4 "The Environment" 27

Epilogue 32

MASTERING THE ART OF INNER PEACE

Prologue 35

Chapter 1 "Who and Why" 38

Chapter 2 "Guidelines to Peace" 41

Chapter 3 "Map to Peace" 43

Chapter 4 "First Stepping Stone" 46

Chapter 5 "Second Stepping Stone" 51

Chapter 6 "Third Stepping Stone" 56

Epilogue 59

MASTERING THE JOY OF SORROW

Prologue 62

Chapter 1 "The Absent Necessity" 65

Chapter 2 "In The Beginning" 70

Chapter 3 "Room For One" 76

Chapter 4 "The Hidden Self" 81

Chapter 5 "World of Weeping" 86

Chapter 6 "Fact and Fantasy" 90

Chapter 7 "Loss and Circumstance" 96

Chapter 8 "The Fragile Soul" 102

Chapter 9 "State of Heart" 110

Chapter 10 "Winds of Change" 114

Chapter 11 "Starting From Scratch" 118

Chapter 12 "Here to There" 121

Chapter 13 "The Inner Storm" 125

Chapter 14 "The Eager Traps" 130

Chapter 15 "The Daily Struggles" 135

Chapter 16 "Timing the Aftermath" 139

Chapter 17 "The Family Connection" 143

Chapter 18 "You Plus One" 147

Chapter 19 "Integration Not Closure" 151

Chapter 20 "The Essential Memories" 155

Chapter 21 "House of Loyalty" 160

Chapter 22 "The New Normal" 164

Chapter 23 "Unknown to All" 168

Chapter 24 "Tale of Woe" 171

Chapter 25 "The Quick Fix" 175

Chapter 26 "The Pet Peeves" 180

Chapter 27 "The Gossip Mill" 185

Chapter 28 "Engineering the Path" 189

Chapter 29 "The Public Prescriptions" 193

Chapter 30 "Risk and Reward" 197

Chapter 31 "Grace Under Fire" 201

Chapter 32 "The Mask Parade" 205

Chapter 33 "The Delicate Dilemma" 209

Chapter 34 "The Patchwork Holidays" 213

Chapter 35 "The Birth Day" 221

Chapter 36 "The Exceptional Legacy" 225

Chapter 37 "The Faith Angle" 230

Chapter 38 "Right and Wrong" 234

Chapter 39 "The Arrogant Airs" 238

Chapter 40 "For Ever More" 242

Epilogue 245

Preface

Grief and bereavement are facets of life none of us escape and can incorporate many diverse losses. Welcome to my personal life story as a bereaved parent.

Forty years ago my first-born, Erin, was suddenly and tragically killed in an accident and now feels the appropriate time for me to honour her and this milestone.

Also, the current state of the world sadly and consistently reflects the myriad of bereaved parents there are throughout the world. A number which seems to be never ending and growing exponentially on a daily basis. A sad reality and one that has also moved me to write this book and share my personal journey from sorrow to joy in an effort to assist in the recovery of the same for others.

The grief journey of a bereaved parent is like no other. It is one often misunderstood by anyone who has not had to endure the experience and all I share is for the benefit of both the bereaved, those looking to support them, and anyone looking to become comfortable with grief.

Everything is meant to support you with the comfort of understanding and a voice of knowledge at your side to shed light on your path. It is a long and arduous journey and the timing of it is yours.

May the information shadow your experience with the confident promise of your ability to return to the very essential joy of life.

Thank you for embracing Our Compatible Grief.

Deborah

Acknowledgements

It is important for me to give thanks to everyone who has supported the process of writing this book.

My 92 year old mother, the very special Ethel Jeffers, tops the list along with my Dad (Fred) though he passed in 2016. Through the years everything that you both taught me will be reflected and obvious to all who travel the pages of this book. I have always felt very blessed to have been placed into your loving arms at birth and I am your product. Thank you Mom and Dad. Please know I am also remembering your little baby Heather who came into this world and left far too soon. I am sorry for that loss you both endured.

To my dear sister, Marsha Jeffers, thank you for all you have contributed to this endeavour. In addition to your investment of time and valuable editing feedback, there are no words that can adequately describe how much I have enjoyed our partnership, as sisters and friends. Your creativity is a blessing and a gift. Thank you Marsha.

To my niece, Meredith Sanders, thank you for your contribution to this beautiful book cover. Living in western Canada, you are blessed with those awesome northern lights and I am thrilled that you chose to share them for this undertaking and giving you credit gives me great pleasure. They are so fitting and beautiful, Thank you, Meredith.

Special credit also goes to my nephew, Gary Conrad Jr, the chapter cover photograph you so generously provided is a wonderful depiction for the chosen topic and destination and also provides an insight into the beauty that is part of western Canada. Thank you, Gary.

There are so many who have supported Our Compatible Grief from beginning to end. Each person in their own way have added value to the project. To my children, Heather, Craig, and Maggie, three of my greatest gifts. I love you. To all of my social media friends ~ you have my love and thanks for the encouragement provided. It has all meant so much.

To my LA team at the Author's Point who shared their expertise to create in their words, the "perfect book", and website, I shall be for ever grateful. Together, we were able to gel and get a big job done. It has been my pleasure to work with each and every one of you. A special shout-out to Fiona, James, and Medlein, my so patient and kind project managers. We should all be proud of these beautiful accomplishments.

Lastly, to my life partner and very best friend, John-Paul Berriman, thank you for still being here and hanging around through this labour of love to honour Erin. My life is blessed by you and the contributions you have provided from your perspective as a Dad whose son also left this world too soon have been so valuable. The mutual understanding we share is a gift I treasure. Your willingness to always be there to answer my multitude of questions I had while writing was a blessing, no matter what time of day or night it was. Thank you JP, I love you!

Introduction

Welcome to Our Compatible Grief. As mentioned in the preface, if you are someone looking to interact with and support bereaved parents ~ wishing to know what to say, what not to say, and how to help ~ this book is for you. If you are a bereaved parent seeking understanding and a way to navigate your grief that works for you and those around you, you've also come to the right place.

Our Compatible Grief is a compilation of what I believe to be the necessary ingredients for the successful completion of the journey from sorrow to joy. Everything shared on these pages has played an integral part in both my healing from the death of my sweet girl, the restoration of my joy of life and the closing of the gap that grief can create between everyone

I am sharing below the layout which reflects the order I would suggest you undertake; however, the book is designed in a way that also allows you to approach it in whatever way speaks to you and in the order you choose. This is your journey and you are in charge.

Initially, Our Compatible Grief will introduce you to a four chapter overview of Mastering the Art of Journaling. Opportunities to journal abound throughout the book and the overview is designed to get you comfortable with the process.

Following that you will have the opportunity to become familiar with a six chapter overview of a three-step process to Mastering

the Art of Inner Peace. Cementing inner peace before approaching the forty chapters of Mastering the Joy of Sorrow would be beneficial but not a necessity.

Lastly, throughout Mastering the Joy of Sorrow in Our Compatible Grief we will explore the bereaved parent's grief journey and how it impacts not only those who grieve but also the broader world. We will delve into the conflicts and challenges that arise, offering a path toward healing and connection for everyone involved.

Our Compatible Grief aims to create understanding and foster growth. It seeks to lift the veil of secrecy that can exist for bereaved parents and explore its dynamics and offer insights to help everyone navigate the complexities of grief. Every chapter in this book has a destination and is written with the trust that they will be reached by each of you over time should you choose to implement the guidance provided into your life. The destinations reflect aspects of my life that needed recovering following the death of my daughter. May the ones that speak to you support your efforts to return to the joy of life.

MASTERING THE ART OF JOURNALING

Prologue

"Believing you have to be a writer or a published author to master the art of journaling is a myth."

Welcome to mastering the art of the journal everyone. Let's have a look at what that means exactly.

Art is defined as being the expression or realm of what may be considered beautiful or appealing, perhaps not so beautiful or of more than ordinary significance.

Journaling is a record of occurrences, experiences, thoughts, feelings and emotions.

There are many opportunities within the confines of the subject matter in Our Compatible Grief where journaling would be a very worthwhile process to undertake. Should you wish to do so, I felt it prudent to share some tips and tools with you around what I believe to be the four components of journaling. The information can be applied to all journaling endeavours, not just those of bereaved parents.

Over the years, when speaking at conferences and working with individuals, it became apparent to me that there was no shortage of people who were discomforted by the prospect of journaling. They considered it writing, which it typically can be; however, they did not see themselves as writers. Being someone who has always enjoyed taking on the debunking of myths and stigmas, I was anxious to put this information together for those of you who believe you have to be a writer in order to successfully journal.

My response to the impression some hold that if you are not a writer you can't journal is quite simple ~

"Forget everything you were ever taught in school relative to writing."

What we learned there relative to writing creates barriers for us in approaching journaling. There really are no common threads between writing and journaling in my view. Journaling does not encompass those rules associated with proper spelling, punctuation, grammar, etc. Those things have absolutely no connection to thoughts, feelings, and emotions. Nor do they have a place in the journaling process. Do not worry, your teacher would forgive you.

Trusting you will find the suggestions provided to be valuable and user-friendly is my wish. Journaling is your process and provides you with the freedom to set it up and execute it however you would like.

It is my pleasure to provide some ideas around what I believe to be conducive to successful journaling and wish you the best of luck!

Chapter 1
"The Journal"

Destination Reflection

Your journal provides the space for you to freely and fearlessly express yourself and is an extension of you. For enhanced success the journal you choose should reflect you. Give careful thought to the following.

Select one of a colour or design you connect with and ensure it is not from your intellect but from your heart and inner essence. Remember, journaling is not an intellectual undertaking.

Select a texture that feels good to you. Close your eyes and experiment with different ones by way of touch.

Decide if you would like a hard cover or not.

Decide if you want a coil-bound one or not. Inside or outside coils are available.

Consider whether you will want to be able to lay it out flat for reading or writing.

There are many sizes of journals available. Pick the one that speaks to you. Consider whether you will only be using it at home or will be taking it elsewhere.

Be sure to check out the texture of the pages carefully to ensure they will work with the materials you are going to select for journaling.

Again, based on materials, decide if you want your journal pages to be lined or not.

Plain or designed cover is up to you. Think about it.

Make sure to read about all four components prior to making your decision and selecting your journal. Develop a sense of what you will be using for materials, the environment, etc. All four should

be conducive to each other and experiencing a connection with each is vital.

Fill the next blank page or two with reminders to yourself about any thoughts that come up for you relative to what kind of journal you think you may like after having considered all of the above. Do so however you like ~ words, drawings, pictures, etc.

Imagine and have fun.

"May you allow the destination of reflection inspire you to step forward."

My Journal Choice Ideas

My Journal Choice Ideas

Chapter 2
"The Mindset"

Destination Privacy

When it comes to a mindset for journaling, we must be willing to be as much like nature in our minds as we can.

There is a long-held belief about the bumblebee. It is not supposed to be able to fly from an aerodynamic perspective and it has been said that it flies anyway, simply because it doesn't know it shouldn't be able to.

Just as bumblebees choose to do what they want, at the speed they want, without restrictions; so must we when journaling. Boundaries limit us and having none allows us to create our own flow, and in so doing, we are rewarded with a huge gift; freedom of expression.

Recall in the welcome, I mentioned school and everything we were taught there relative to writing. A complete memory erase of all those rules learned is encouraged by me for the purpose of journaling. None of it matters in this arena.

Should you be someone who does not possess strong literacy or writing skills, fear not. You can successfully journal. Journaling can be achieved in easy fashion as you will come to learn by the time you have reached the end of these tips and tools.

Do not concern yourself with whether there is a right or wrong anything. Journaling is not about right or wrong. It is about where you are at in your life in any given moment in time. It is about your thoughts, feelings, and emotions connected to your life experiences and events; not anything else.

Journaling is and can be very therapeutic. It gives us a place to put things that are taking up space inside us; thereby, making

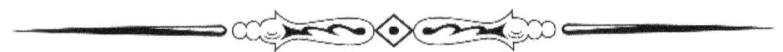

room available there for new and perhaps more positive things. It is also a great measuring stick of progress for us when we have life events we are working through. Reflecting back on our journal entries will always reveal to us just how far we have come, when perhaps we are not able to see it or feel it on a day-to-day basis.

Should you be someone who will pick writing as your mode of journaling, do not concern yourself with whether it is in sentences or only a list of words. Either works. You are the only one who needs to comprehend their meaning. You don't even have to use words. You can create your own code if you like.

This is your journal containing your most private and intimate thoughts, feelings, and emotions. It is up to you whether you choose to share it or not. If you don't wish to share, simply explain "It is my journal. It is a private matter."

In efforts to help you develop the right mindset for undertaking the art of journaling, I would encourage you to think about what might be preventing you from giving it a try.

Is it something you have considered in the past but never did it?

If so, why was that?

Use the following page or two to list any barriers you believe might be in the way of you journaling. Again, using whatever format and materials speak to you.

Mindset matters!

"May you allow the destination of privacy inspire you to step forward."

My Mindset Barriers

My Mindset Barriers

Chapter 3
"The Materials"

Destination Creativity

The materials available for use and which are allowed when journaling are limitless. Let your imagination run free and know no bounds.

Use materials that inspire and motivate you. As was mentioned in Chapter 1, The Journal, your materials are also an extension of you and should reflect your inner essence.

You can write, print, draw, paint, colour; whatever you want.

No matter which utensil you choose, pay attention and make sure it feels good in your hand and glides effortlessly across the paper in your journal.

You can use stickers and there are a wide and diverse assortment of those in the marketplace. Ones that are expressive of what and how you feel are also common. You can use markers, coloured pencils, pens, pencils, crayons. By the way, using crayons creates safety for us.

Use colour freely. All colours have meanings and can aid in readily expressing certain emotions and feelings.

ORANGE is a balancing colour for us. Remember, it is a combination of red and yellow. It will bring out the kid in you, the playfulness. It can lower the feeling of being bored and give us a sense of balance. Your artist energy will be activated.

BLUE is relaxing and can be calming. Using blue can make communication easy with self or others. If you are going to write a letter to someone in your journal, blue would be a good choice. Peace and understanding will come with using blue and get you in touch with your spiritual side.

YELLOW is a colour we almost immediately associate with the sun. It is an energetic colour and positively impacts our body, especially in a healing way. It can clarify your thoughts and assist in taking them from a state of confusion to one of order. It can also improve your memory and will connect you to your wisdom.

GREEN brings feelings of harmony, health, and of course, abundance. Green is the only colour apart from all others for which our eyes are able to recognize the most variation. It is the colour of growth and expansion and connects us to life and nature.

RED is an energy and power colour. It will ignite our passion, interest level, and enthusiasm; while providing a sense of security at the same time. It will be a kick us into gear colour and creates in us a desire for activity. It is nourishing to the physical self.

Use colour from both the perspective of how you are feeling and from the perspective of thoughts, feelings, and emotions you want to engage.

Be creative!

Take ownership!

Be artistic!

Express yourself!

Make it all about you!

Have fun!

Be fearless!

Use the next page or two for experimenting with colours and utensils. Play around and discover which you enjoy using the most, and which feel the best to you. Find out which ones you connect with. Check them all out ~ draw, paint, write, colour, use stickers.

"May you allow the destination of creativity inspire you to step forward."

My Materials Ideas

My Materials Ideas

Chapter 4
"The Environment"

Destination Calm

When choosing your journaling environment, it, too, is an extension of you and your inner essence. Therefore, you should give some consideration to the environmental aspects of you.

Are you someone who loves nature or are you the curl up in front of the fire type?

Which is your preference? Inside, outside, or both?

What soothes and inspires you at the same time? For me it is the ocean.

Are you a day or night time being?

Preparing to journal can be likened to getting ready to entertain someone for dinner. Creating the atmosphere is not only fun but it is also directly related to the level of success that will be achieved.

There are a few tips I would like to recommend for your process of creating an optimum environment in which to journal.

Wear really comfy clothing. Pyjamas and sweats work well.

Music softly playing in the background is often helpful. You get to choose what music. Instrumentals are usually very soothing and relaxing. A tune I particularly enjoy and find works well is Always With You, Always With Me by Joe Satriani.

Create lighting which is beneficial to the process, yet not harsh. Light some candles too.

Location is important. Pick a spot that resonates with you. You can have more than one if you like.

Schedule a time that will be quiet and uninterrupted. Life can be very busy so you may just want to slot it in the same way you schedule other events in your life. Knowing that in advance and

thinking about what you are going to journal about ahead of time assists in putting you in the zone when the time comes. Scheduling is not an absolute necessity but doing so will aid in building your consistent commitment to the process and lessen those procrastination tendencies.

Have a beverage handy. You get to choose.

Use the following page or two to simulate your desired environment. You can glue pictures here. Again utilize whatever format you wish. Imagine how you see yourself when journaling and create a visual of it for you. It can be a wonderful motivator in getting you there. Create more than one if you like. Perhaps one for each season, one for day, one for night, inside or outside. There are many options available to you.

Where can you see yourself?

"May you allow the destination of calm inspire you to step forward."

My Perfect Environment Ideas

My Perfect Environment Ideas

Epilogue

"Never fear creativity. Being creative is a sign you are alive and living life."

In ending this addition to Our Compatible Grief, it is my wish everything shared has helped to paint a picture for you of the art of journaling.

When you weave the four components together you will have everything you need in place to be comfortable with the process. An example for you of incorporating all four components might look like this.

If you love the ocean, you may be inclined to purchase a journal that has a picture of the ocean on it or one that has a gritty sand textured cover. Perhaps it will have blue pages or maybe your utensil colours will be predominantly blue. Sitting on the beach in warm comfy sweats with a favourite beverage beside you completes the picture.

By having participated in the exercises included after each of the four component chapters, you have experienced journaling on a small scale.

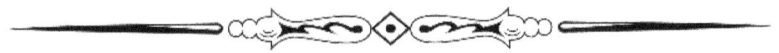

I am confident after having done so, you will be looking forward to honing your journaling skills and approach the habit with excitement. I use the word habit because once you have mastered the art, it becomes habit. One that I trust you will come to love as much as I do.

I am an advocate of my quote at the top of this page and encourage you to create your plan in your mind and on the pages provided with each component, allow it to excite you, then share your plan to journal with others if you want and it will happen for you.

MASTERING THE ART OF INNER PEACE

Prologue

"When what is being projected outside self is not aligned with what is happening inside self, know there is a need for inner peace restoration."

Inner peace is something that has been in place for me most of my life and has played a critical role in my grief journey as a bereaved Mom. Mastering inner peace is an undertaking I believe every person on the planet deserves. Bereaved or not.

I am happy to share what I know to be true about inner peace with the intention of it being of interest or service to others who are longing to have it and would like to get it back.

My core beliefs around inner peace have always been with me and should you ask me where they came from, I would not have an answer for you, other than perhaps my childhood experiences with polio which provided ample opportunities for quiet introspection. They have served me well throughout my lifetime and I have always viewed them as a gift of sorts.

The process of attaining inner peace and then sustaining it comes more easily to some than others and I believe those who have it are the teachers for those who want it. Even as long as mine has been with me, rest assured throughout the

years I have had teachers, remained open, learned, and will always be grateful to them. The wisdom of others is a wonderful gift during those times when the rough waters of life can remove a person from their true self.

What is Inner Peace?

Inner peace is all about me, the person. The journey to mastering the art of inner peace and the journey to joy for the bereaved parent are the only two occasions I have had experience with when I have ever thought anything should be all about me. They were the only two occasions also when it needed to be that way.

For me, personally, it is something that is quite separate from my life, from what happens in my life, or what is going on outside of myself and in the world. Those things are connected to my outer peace, which is divergent. Separation of the two, inner and outer peace, is crucial.

Inner peace must be up and running and anchored securely first, as it is designed to be the driver for the management of outer peace. At least that has been my experience.

Contrary to popular belief, inner peace is not something you go looking to find or spend time searching for; it is something you rediscover from within. Right from where you sit, stand, or lay.

The rediscovery of inner peace requires the desire and ability to be honest with self about self. It is the development of a

single being who behaves consistently and in a manner that allows everyone else to be very clear on who we are, in any location and under any circumstances. We are a constant. Achieving that state requires a candid look at self and it is hard work. The process may not always be pretty and can reveal things we may not be particularly proud of recognizing and accepting; however, we must.

When it comes to outer peace, that is much more difficult to master because there are mega contributors to what goes on outside of us. It is even more difficult to master when inner peace is not in place and in good working order. The upside is we are not bothered by those mega contributors so much anymore and become capable of handling them much more efficiently when a strong foundation of inner peace becomes the CEO of our life, if you will.

I believe life should always be approached, in every aspect, from the inside out. After all, that is how we came into being in the first place from our Mother's womb.

Take pride should you choose to immerse yourself in this process. You are worthy of the benefits you will reap and the formula is quite simple.

TRUTH + COURAGE = INNER PEACE

Chapter 1
"Who and Why"

Destination Discovery

Mastering the Art of Inner Peace is for every single person who is feeling deprived of being at peace with self. There is no special criteria needed. We can all fit the bill.

Out of all those people, though, it is for those who are ready, willing, and able to shift what may be a current perspective of searching for inner peace to one of creating inner peace. It is NOT something found anywhere. All the ingredients needed exist inside you.

This process can be stopped, started and then returned to at any time. You are in charge. There is no established time frame attached.

You will step in when your desire to achieve its purpose becomes greater than any fears you may have associated with taking it on.

May this process provide some assistance, give you a starting point and with hard work and commitment from you, inner peace will be your reward.

Why do I want to share my thoughts on mastering the art of inner peace?

I have had the pleasure of being a resident on planet Earth for well over half a century and most especially in the past twenty-five years I have observed a decline in the number of people who are enjoying the benefits of inner peace. It simply does not appear to me to exist for many; though I stand to be corrected, no problem.

I grew up with the old adage and the song "this little light of mine, I'm gonna let it shine". Look it up if it is not familiar to you. The concept of this little light seems to have disappeared into the night or somewhere else. Without some semblance of inner peace activated, a person is unable to let their light shine.

There are tons of human facades out there, no shortage of those. How very unfortunate. There is a direct correlation between inner peace and happiness; just as there is a direct correlation between facades and unhappiness. At least I believe that to be true.

Let's have a look at the world in current day. We are so very technologically connected and so humanly disconnected. Diversity reigns. Suicides are up. Crime rates are up. Dysfunctional families can be found around the globe. Divorce is up.

Greed and corruption abound.

I believe the lack of or non-existence of inner peace causes a lowering of consciousness and where there is low to no consciousness, the chances of successful outcomes to anything are impaired, if not altogether impossible.

I trust my road map to inner peace that follows will contribute to changing some of what I have shared.

I love people and believe we each deserve peace, serenity, and happiness. I also know it begins with each of us and flourishes from there. Remember the equation truth + courage = inner peace.

"May you allow the destination of discovery inspire you to step forward."

Chapter 2
"Guidelines to Peace"

Destination Insight

Below are my recommended guidelines for you as you begin your journey to mastering the art of inner peace. There are only six and I really cannot stress enough the importance of you giving each of them serious consideration accompanied by the knowledge they are all vital to your success.

Some of them may create discomfort for you; however, as I often say, getting comfortable with being uncomfortable is a required part of the process. You may feel vulnerable and perhaps fear. As adverse as you know these feelings can be, I would encourage you to receive the gift of freedom they can bring to you when faced. You will survive them, not to worry.

Simply know

1. You are participating in a non-judgmental process.

2. Honesty to and with self and others is necessary.

3. Sharing and interactions with others is required.

4. A willingness to being open to what others say is critical.

5. You must not take anything personally or take offence.

6. Arm yourself up with paper or journal and your favourite writing utensil, not a computer.

Memorize the formula: truth + courage = inner peace.

"May you allow the destination of insight inspire you to move forward."

Chapter 3
"Map to Peace"

Destination Transparency

Kindly give some thought to this for a moment. Have you ever noticed how life has a way of taking us from all that we may have hoped for, planned for, or dreamed of while growing up? Can you recall those days of childhood when our imagination was so active, our possibilities were endless, and we believed we were capable of just about anything?

Those hopes, plans, and dreams we had as children were a reflection of our true self at a time in our lives when inner peace was part of us and play a central role in our return to it. The road map reveals our inner peace place is both the starting point and the destination. To get there, we must travel back in time before we are able to forge ahead to rediscover it.

Doing so involves working back through what was heaped upon us that has developed in us behaviours and symptoms that are preventing us from the renewal of our true inner peace self. Three stepping stones in the form of written exercises for you to work through are all it takes for most people and they are shared as you move through this process.

I am sharing some examples for you that are indicative of a lacking in the area of inner peace. Should you connect to any of them, consider them triggers for you as something that should perhaps be given attention. Try not to analyze them or write them off as insignificant. I would encourage you to highlight any with which you may connect.

It is imperative to be totally honest to and with yourself

I am unable to enjoy a healthy and consistent sleep pattern.

I have a poor memory.

I am unable to feel calm and zone into just me.

I have an impending sense of doom and gloom.

I lack courage and can be fearful.

I have regrets.

I am sick and tired ~ of feeling sick and tired.

I am unable to just relax and be at ease.

I am unable to dispel my anger.

I often feel like I am on a roller coaster.

I am often anxious and stressed.

I am unwelcoming of views or feelings of another.

I am so busy doing things for others I cannot get to my own.

Never forget: truth + courage = inner peace.

"May you allow the destination of transparency inspire you to step forward."

Chapter 4
"First Stepping Stone"

Destination Clarity

Now that you have had the opportunity to become aware of what may pertain to you, it is time to move into the stepping stone exercises. This is where the real work begins, so put your hard hat on; white, of course because you are the supervisor of this endeavour. You are the engineer of your own life; which could be likened to the little engine that could. A huge pay off awaits.

Let's get started.

Please read the full instructions for this exercise before starting the work. Have your pen/paper/journal nearby.

This exercise will involve both yourself and the input of others. As previously mentioned in the guidelines; as you involve others in this process, it will be necessary for you to share honestly with them what it is you are working on and ask their permission to have them participate.

Points to Consider

Ensure your others are those who have a clear understanding of the deep and personal commitment you are making and clarify for them the need for the high level of respect required for its confidential nature.

Are they someone who is truly ready, willing, and able to participate in the honest manner that is required? Ask them.

Ensure they understand the importance of their most brutal honesty and also ensure the same of yourself.

Let them know that whatever they wish to share is going to be received by you without judgment.

Be selective in whom you invite to participate. People we trust who are willing to speak the truth are the best prospects.

Page Set Up

1. Take your sheet of paper or your journal and set it up in the following way:

2. At the top of the page, print your full name in BIG BLOCK LETTERS.

3. Draw a vertical line at centre of page from top to bottom creating two equal columns.

4. Create an I AM header at the top of the left column.

5. Create a YOU ARE header at the top of the right column.

Writing Instructions

In the I AM column, write down all the qualities you have that YOU love about yourself. Not behaviours, only character traits. Some examples would be honesty, compassion, sense of humour.

You may discover there are some you have not utilized in a while and that is okay. They may be ones that you believe are true about yourself yet, for whatever reason, you have been unable to reveal to others. That, too, is okay and they should be included in your list. Also include any qualities that you feel you are capable of; though, perhaps, have been lost along the way or maybe even have not yet mastered. Ones you wish to develop or rediscover.

Remember, you are on a journey to reconnect yourself with the true you. Use one word descriptors only. Some examples to help you get started are such things as intelligent, teachable, creative, etc.

Give yourself credit for what you know you have inside you, possibly screaming to get out! At this moment, it is just you and your writing. Be good to you.

In the YOU ARE column, you are going to write down everything others say they love about you when you ask them. You may come to find there are attributes others experience with you that perhaps you are not even conscious of and they can be very enlightening and empowering, to say the least. Be accepting of all that others bring to you. Be gracious and do not argue. Allow your esteem and worth receive all you deserve. You can involve as many people as you want.

Once completed, take some quality time to compare, peruse, and ponder the two lists. Contemplate each quality carefully and determine which ones truly resonate with you.

Are you able to allow yourself to understand why another would see something that perhaps you don't? Does it feel like you? There is no right or wrong, only truth.

Next Step

Highlight all the qualities from both columns you believe are reflective of the real you and then give thought to your use of them in daily life.

Mark with an H the ones that are hidden from the outside world or an R if they are ones that are revealed. This can be a point in the

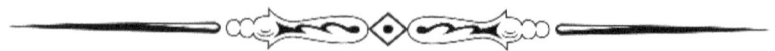

process where you may decide to give some thought as to why each were identified as hidden or revealed.

In Conclusion

To complete this first stepping stone exercise, go to a new sheet of paper and create a new I AM list which will be a compilation of all the qualities provided by both you and others. Those ones you have come to recognize and accept as being reflective of the true you. Post it somewhere so it may serve as a daily reminder to you. Read it daily, verbalize it out loud in front of a mirror if you want. Doing so can be very powerful.

Continue this practice daily until it becomes so embedded within your being that you won't need to look at it anymore. When that happens for you, it is a sign you have taken ownership and are beginning to enjoy a clearer understanding of all that you are never to be intruded upon again either by you or anyone else.

Remember the formula! Recall once more, truth + courage = inner peace.

"May you allow the destination of clarity inspire you to step forward."

Chapter 5
"Second Stepping Stone"

Destination Elimination

Once again, please read the full instructions for this exercise before starting and have your pen/paper/journal nearby.

In order to develop inner peace, it is key to be ready, willing, and able to give as much credence to what is not loved about you by both yourself and others as we gave to what is loved.

What is not loved is typically manifested in behaviours whereas what is loved manifests in the form of qualities or character traits.

It is our life experiences which create behaviours that may not be attractive and we should not allow them to deviate us from our true self, although it happens that's for sure and more often than we like or want. It is easy to get so busy with life we may not even be aware that they do. Creating inner peace takes care of them to our advantage as opposed to our disadvantage.

Points to Consider

Again, I want to stress the importance of brutal honesty by both yourself and others. It is critical for this exercise as well and the same conditions apply as previously shared.

This portion of the process can be one of the more difficult. You may find yourself feeling vulnerable. You may find yourself brought to tears. You may experience churnings of anger or feeling offended. I urge you to labour through it. Stay focused on your goal of creating inner peace and reaping its rewards. Imagine how that will feel and allow it to be your inspiration.

Page Set Up

1. Take your sheet of paper or your journal and set it up in the following way:

2. At the top of the page, print your full name in BIG BLOCK LETTERS.

3. Draw a vertical line on the page from top to bottom creating two equal columns.

4. Create an I DO header at the top of the left column.

5. Create a YOU DO header at the top of the right column.

Writing Instructions

In your I DO column, make a list of all the behaviours your exhibit to self and others that you do not love. These are the ones that plague you, that clog your mind, that keep you awake at night and perhaps cause you to stay busy doing nothing or doing for others in the hopes of avoiding having to think about them.

Some examples would be deceiving others, using people or taking advantage, playing the victim, lying, being self-centred, owing money, and so on. Remember, negative behaviours are usually a reflection of where we are (our circumstances), not who we are.

In the YOU ARE column, you will write the list of behaviours that others see and experience with you that they do not love and have shared with you. Again, it is necessary for you to be ready, willing, and able to be open to receiving this perspective of others. We should never underestimate the value of recognizing and accepting

the impact we have upon someone else. Without knowing what the impact is, how would we ever be able to decide whether or not it is reflective of our true self? We can't.

Bear in mind that although a behaviour may be one that is not loved by self or others; as you journey back clearing your path to the place of inner peace, some of them may be ones that can become valuable assets once adjusted and used in the proper vein. When that happens they will have a different name and bring to you different outcomes; such as a clear conscience.

Next Step

Again, as in the previous exercise, take the time to contemplate everything that has been revealed by both yourself and others. Consider each behaviour carefully and highlight everything you are willing to take ownership of and forgive yourself for when required.

Remember, no time is to be invested in right or wrong, only truth as ugly as it may look to you. Again, mark those with an H that are hidden and those revealed with an R. Do not give any consideration to whether they are hidden or revealed to only you or how many other people. When they are hidden from or revealed to only one person, it is of significance.

In Conclusion

Take a new sheet of paper and create your new I DO list of behaviours you have owned up to that is a compilation of what is not loved by you and others.

Make the decision to never behave in those ways again. Tell yourself out loud I am never _____ again with each and every one of them.

Then destroy the sheet of paper. You can ball it up and throw it away. Burn it. Tear it up. Whatever your want. You don't need it anymore. They will no longer serve the purpose they once did as you have now determined which ones are not connected to your true self.

You are doing great with the formula truth +courage = inner peace.

"May you allow the destination of elimination inspire you to step forward."

Chapter 6
"Third Stepping Stone"

Destination Light

By now your picture of you should be showing itself with an improved and honest clarity. One that represents who you truly are and with the knowledge of what you truly don't want or need. It is a picture that has not been experienced by the outside world because you have not yet completed your third and final stepping stone exercise. It can be a tough one, perhaps the toughest of all.

What is left for you to accomplish?

It is the removal of the camouflage and masquerades. Those masks that prevent honesty with yourself and others are no longer needed and are waiting to be removed. They are part of what has enslaved you. You have completed your behind the masks work and the shedding of them requires pure courage. Shedding them will create freedom for you and resistance from others. Are you up for it? Once you remove them the world will only see the new, true, and real you from here on out.

It can be very difficult to show the world that person, especially if you are someone who has spent years creating an image or reputation that you believe the world thinks you should be living up to.

Most people tend to pay more heed to their reputation than their character. Lots of people believe they are one and the same. Not so. Inner peace becomes the underlying building block to character. You can build a false reputation; however, you cannot build false character. Character will withstand anything. Reputation will not.

Is it really worth it to continue down that path of reputation when you may not be experiencing any inner peace or level of happiness worth mention? My personal opinion would be I think not. However, it is up to you. It is a personal choice.

Those masks, which are invisible to others, and perhaps even to our own conscious self are nothing but burdensome.

All the information shared in these three stepping stone exercises is very connected and they each require you to shift perspective in order to get back to you.

The steps serve as your new three r's:

RECOGNITION	~ of what has separated you from your inner peace
REMOVAL	~ of those pieces that do not apply
REIGNITION	~ of those traits reflective of your true self

As always, truth + courage = inner peace.

"May you allow the destination of light inspire you to step forward."

Epilogue

"Getting comfortable with the rawness of your true core self will bring you home to where the inner peace place is waiting for you. Congratulations on letting yourself back in!"

There are many rewards to be reaped when living with self-sustaining inner peace. I can only speak with credibility to the ones I have enjoyed through the years and consider myself fortunate and blessed. It is my wish that you come to enjoy the same.

Available Rewards

Your need or desire to glean anything from another is eradicated.

You are able to stand your ground in any situation with conviction.

You are able to place your head on the pillow at night and enjoy rest and relaxation.

You have the ability to stand and survive; either alone or with another should you choose to share your life.

You become freed up from the exhausting multi-behaviour syndrome that our own self or the world often feels is necessary or seems to expect.

You develop a very clear understanding of what is and is not appropriate and acceptable to you and can articulate that to others without fear of repercussions. You know you will manage whatever comes your way.

You become the master of you and no longer need to be the master of deception, greed, arrogance, cowardice, charm and so on.

You are free from the ties that once bound you.

You are consistent and reliable in your thoughts, words, and actions.

~ and last but not least ~

Your honest self, whom you will become quite comfortable with, will never again have to remember a thing you have spoken. You will not have to concern yourself with anyone using your spoken word against you because with all the rewards in place, you and your truth speak for themselves and you are protected; simply by being you.

"May blessings of light, love, joy and inner peace be yours always!"

MASTERING THE JOY OF SORROW

Prologue

"One of the key ingredients to building advocacy and inclusion in the world is empathy. Sympathy will not."

Mastering the Joy of Sorrow will explore those aspects of the bereaved parent grief journey that produce conflict and chaos for everyone and look at the challenges that percolate for both grievers and everyone else. They all play a role in causing us to grow distant from each other.

For those who may not have ever considered the existence of what I call a club for bereaved parents perhaps because in the outside world there is no reason to consider such a thing, kindly allow me to acquaint you. The truth is there is no official club; however, there certainly exists what I call the unofficial club to which all bereaved parents hold membership. It is very private, exclusive, and not always discussed. It can quite often be a secret.

I don't believe there can be any secrets attached to the expectation of a successful outcome to any endeavour; therefore, I shall reveal all I experienced as a bereaved Mom. Hidden agendas never contribute to success in any undertaking so let's go behind the scenes and reveal the club.

Membership in this club is not optional. There are no special requirements, skills, educational, religious, or cultural criteria one has to meet to become a member. Its membership is unparalleled, encompassing people from all walks of life. There are no borders or boundaries. I would be safe in saying this club has attained the highest levels of inclusion and diversity, bar none. Selection is by circumstance, not by choice or anything else and anyone could be a member of the club instantaneously. We have the quickest registration process of any club known to man. It is a lifetime membership. Its cost is exorbitant yet no money ever exchanges hands. Membership in this club, while uninvited, can offer connection, growth, and even purpose for those willing to embrace its lessons.

Before we journey further, let me validate what it took for you to open this book. By doing so, you have already provided three profound gifts to yourself and others.

The first gift is courage. Grief is an arena no one chooses to enter, yet here you are revealing a willingness to face its challenges. Your courage inspires others to step into this space with you.

The second gift is openness. The grief journey is long, painful, and deeply personal. By remaining open to learning and sharing, you create space for growth—for yourself and for those who walk this path with you.

The third gift is time. Time is the most valuable gift we can give to ourselves and others. Your investment of time to understanding, healing, and building joy again is a testament to your resilience.

For those of us in this club, everything has changed. The world we once knew is gone, replaced by a new reality that requires us to rebuild trust—in ourselves, in others, and in life itself. This journey is not linear and it demands patience, compassion, and strength.

This book is an invitation to walk the path together. As we journey side by side, we will learn from one another and find ways to rebuild what has been shattered. Letting go of the old and embracing the new is not easy, but it is necessary. This process,

though painful, holds the promise of transformation and renewed hope.

Immerse yourself into these chapters designed to provide knowledge for the non-griever and messages for the bereaved Moms and Dads. May Our Compatible Grief be a guide and a comfort, helping us all embrace the shared human experience of loss and the possibility of joy. Doing so would be refreshingly reminiscent of simpler times when joining forces did not mean there was a war somewhere but rather a joining of humanity. Heart-to-heart, hand-in-hand, and face-to-face.

Let our journey back to joy begin.

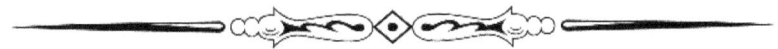

Chapter 1
"The Absent Necessity"

Destination Joy

When I use the word joy I am referring to the joy of life. As bereaved parents when one of our children dies, our joy of life is an aspect that is also taken, can be lost for a time and needs to be recaptured.

I was made keenly aware of the absence of joy in just a short few hours upon the death of Erin. On the night of Erin's death when it came time to put her little sister Heather to bed in the room they had shared, one of my most treasured memories of joy came flooding back all on its own. About a week before Erin died as I was tucking her in for the night and doing our hugs and kisses she had asked me "Mommy, will you always kiss and hug me good night?" to which I replied "Of course, for always." Then she brought me that beautiful gift of joy by saying "Oh, I'm so glad because you know it is one of my favourite things." "It is one of my favourite things, too" I replied. Little did I know in that moment how quickly the joy and love I received nightly was going to change and by how much and that it would be in an instant. It disappeared.

That evening of her death and every night after for a very long time I was tormented by the pain that memory conjured up for me as opposed to the joy it had used to provide. Instead of being accompanied by smiles it was now accompanied by tears. How I missed those small arms and hands wrapping themselves around me and squeezing me so very tightly.

Joy could be defined as a source or cause of pleasure or delight, an emotion or state of happiness or to be glad or rejoice. Sadly, there is no plethora of true joy in the world by today's standards; however, I believe there needs to be as it is what makes everything worthwhile.

It is one of the greatest inspirations to bless a person. The levels of pain, heartache, and devastation in the world could be greatly

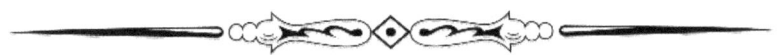

diminished with a healthy infusion of joy. Just imagine what a breath of fresh air that would be.

It can feel as though joy is nowhere to be found upon the death of our child. Joy is the absent, yet so necessary, destination for the bereaved and this book is designed to assist moving everyone from pain and sorrow back to joy and happiness. By everyone I mean bereaved Moms and Dads, surviving siblings of the child who has died, extended family members, and those I refer to as the outside world folks. Our work colleagues, friends, clergy, neighbours, etc. Joy is a critical and necessary element of life and we are all deserving of its return and presence in our lives. Let's take a look at how important it is in our daily life.

When we contemplate the personal experiences with joy we have delighted in, we recognize it comes to us from a variety of sources. Our children, no doubt, would be one source. Also our spouse/partner, jobs, schooling, church, friends and neighbours, family members, nature, just to name a few. Downtime activities such as taking a drive, reading, love, travel, movies, and volunteer work have also contributed to our experiences with joy. The list is limitless.

Let me use a friend as a comparison analogy for you to relate to in efforts to build an awareness for everyone of the difference between a friend leaving our life, whether by death or not, and one of our children dying.

I am trusting it is safe to presume that most, if not all of us, have had at least one friend who is no longer in our life for whatever reason. Reflecting back upon their leaving, we may notice the loss of joy they had brought to us. At the same time we recognize their loss has not negatively impacted the elements of joy being brought to us by other sources. We remain the recipients of those. However, the death of our child can negatively impact the joy from

every source. They all disappear or so it can feel that way to us, the grieving parents.

When our hearts are hurting, we may very well be broke but we are not broken. A truth we may not realize for a very long time. It is very easy for us to fall into the "i am broken" mode. It is what we feel and one of many things we have absolutely no control over so please do not be shocked to hear those words and see that behaviour from us.

Our ability to accept from others what used to bring joy has been suspended for a time along with our ability to bring joy to others. Everyone loses, struggles, and suffers with this aspect of a bereaved parent's grief and is deserving of awareness and respect from others.

An acknowledgement from others who are looking to support us in our absence of joy is always appreciated.

"A special message for Moms and Dads"

It would not be unusual for us, bereaved parents, to be in a place where we are no longer confident in the faith that we are even allowed to experience joy in any area of our lives; therefore, we may be contributing to the denial of it for us. Along with our confidence leaving us, so with it may go our beliefs we may have held of joy ever being a part of our lives in the future. This may or may not be anything we are cognizant of as we attempt to navigate our grief journey. It is not intentional on our part. It simply happens and is one of the components of our new reality.

With respect to the issue of joy we used to bring to others, it is true a person can only give to another what they have in place for self. We may no longer be able to provide it for a time and that inability can be easily misconstrued by others. Everyone should be

sensitive to this piece of our journey. Again, awareness by all is critical and beneficial.

The disappearance of joy in our life requires us to first recognize its absence and contemplate what is needed in order for restoration. Does it even still mean anything to us or is its return going to look and feel completely different? Can what used to bring joy still do that even though the one who brought it to us is gone?

For many, many years I felt robbed by the loss of those nightly kisses and hugs. I have come to learn that not only was it the physicality of the interaction that I missed but the benefit being provided to me. My need for joy was no longer being filled. Over time I reformatted my life by taking ownership of the fact that joy was a must for me and worked to discover new ways of having it back in my life. Along with the loss of the person we loved so very much, quite often it is what they brought to us that we are truly missing and becomes the greater hurdle to overcome. What we are missing can be difficult to restore if we have not even recognized that it may be the source of the pain in conjunction with the presence of our loved one being gone. The gift to me in having done so has been the return of that very treasured memory without the pain. Once again, it brings smiles as was the original intent.

When the time arrives for us to make a decision to work through our grief, heal the pain, and become willing to accept and embrace the new you; only then can we begin the journey forward to the joy destination. Trust me when I say everything necessary to make it happen resides inside of you, though I am very aware it may not feel like that to you right now.

> ***"May you allow the destination of joy inspire you to step forward."***

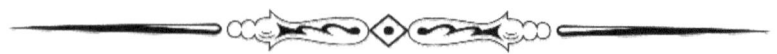

Chapter 2
"In The Beginning"

Destination Freedom

On Thursday, December 6th, 1984 I was working in a local shopping centre as the Marketing and Promotions Manager. We had a beautiful and huge Christmas tree on display in centre court and it was our angel tree. It was hung with angel shaped tags for needy children and we were working toward having the public purchase the requested gifts to be donated to the cause.

I clearly remember being seated at the table by the tree waiting for the mall patrons who would be angels to the needy children when I looked up to see my very close and dear friend who was also my caregiver for the girls moving quickly toward me. It was after 2:30 in the afternoon so I was puzzled because school was out and wondered who was taking care of the children. She informed me that there had been an accident and Erin was on her way to the hospital and we needed to go there. I asked her if Erin was alright and she said she did not know. It was a defining moment in my life. One of those I knew I would never forget and the remainder of that day provided many, many more.

I began to climb the stairs to my office and as I reached the third step, as though it were yesterday, I turned back to her and said "She is dead, isn't she?" and once more the answer was "I don't know". But I did. What came to me was so clear I told her there was really no rush so I was going to take time to make a couple of phone calls before we headed in to the hospital.

The first call was to my husband to ask him to meet me at the hospital and the second call was to our pediatrician whose office was close to the hospital and who I knew would go over immediately. That way, on the off chance Erin was still alive, someone she knew would be there until we arrived. That call to the doctor was my last very fine thread of hope I was holding on to for Erin's survival as I was not wanting to face what I was feeling.

Upon arriving at the hospital, instead of being in the public waiting room, we were immediately escorted into a private room. An immediate red flag for me. Within minutes, our doctor came in and she was looking so uncharacteristically dishevelled I felt as though my worst nightmare was about to be confirmed. She informed us that she had brought in doctors from six different floors in the hospital to emergency and collectively they had worked on Erin for 45 minutes to no avail. She had not survived.

When I was confronted with the news of my Erin's death, I struggled with two thoughts that quickly came to the fore. Immediate consideration had to be given to not only what do I do now, but also what am I supposed to do now. Those thoughts were catapulted into my life when the doctor followed up informing us of her death with asking if we would like to go see her. My husband said yes, I said no. Then I asked the doctor if not wanting to go see her made me a bad Mother. She told me that I had never been a bad Mother and whatever decision I made was okay. My husband went to see Erin and then I found myself asking the doctor if Heather should go to the funeral. I was in foreign territory and felt so disconnected from all that had been my life just a short time ago. We then were having to navigate the decisions around organ donations to which a chapter is devoted later in the book. In the midst of all of this, we still did not know what had happened to her other than the accident involved her schoolbus and she had been too damaged to survive, save, or donate.

Very quickly I came to realize that everything I had chosen to buy into prior to this life altering event no longer applied. Especially the rules society implores us to follow. I was devastated. My world had become simply complex. Was I going to follow the rules or not? That was the only choice being provided. At this point my head was pounding, I was sad and angry, and feeling very overwhelmed.

I was now an official bereaved Mom and as such, gave myself permission to think for self and decided there were no established rules of grief and I have been for ever grateful for having made that decision. Doing so provided a catalyst to moving forward. It also allowed me to see that the rules of the world would only impede the grief process as it is one that can only be navigated in company with tons of thinking and sadly thinking for self is not a concept always embraced by society in current day.

There are stages of grief but there cannot be any rules of grief as the journey is different and unique for every single person.

"A special message for Moms and Dads"

The grief process for a bereaved parent is one for which we must take the lead. This is not to negate resources with great suggestions that are available to us; however, it should always be remembered they may or may not apply to everyone.

The only thoughts I can suggest for beginning this journey and that I have any credibility to speak to are the ones that were mine. The ones that worked for me. I am going to share them and if any strike a chord for you, feel free to take them, apply them to your situation and tweak so they fit your circumstance and loss. Tweaking is necessary because no two people grieve the same, and no two situations are exact ever. There may be common threads but no replicas.

One common thread all of us face is the need to open self up to the reality that our journey back to joy will require us to recreate self. Understanding that was a very unwelcome reality for me. One which changed everything and everyone. Much work is required for us to recognize, accept and not be fearful of the new you which is now in the works. A new you that may be liked or not is yet to

be revealed. We have become a mystery to self and others yet to be solved.

Our grief is a piece meal process with many, many components and each chapter in this book is dedicated to them.

When considering these thoughts, bear in mind that there are two old adages at play here. The truth hurts and more importantly, the one I would really encourage you to focus on; the truth will set you free. You will find this book revealing no-nonsense yet common sense truths.

Truth is the path to freedom and the simplest route although often the path of most resistance. Freedom is the path to joy, peace and serenity. Welcome to some thoughts that are straightforward and implementation of them can act as catalysts for you in moving forward. Establish your path and call it "I Did It My Way" as that is how it must be.

Take care of you first. Remember, when you are in a low, any expectation you may have of being of service to others is fiction. Be honest with your own self first, and then with others. Do not concern yourself with what may be deemed socially acceptable. Know there is no social protocol when it comes to grief. Engage in time only in the manner you can manage. Determine if that is minute by minute, hour by hour, day by day. All are okay. Identify your most immediate need. Take care of it and the next one will reveal itself or you will discover it. Work on only one at a time. Do not worry or be fearful of losing any of your treasured memories of your loved one when you make the decision to move forward. Trust me, when the work is complete, they miraculously shine brighter than ever.

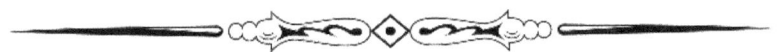

Our grief is work and the only person who can get you through it is you. Allow the word freedom to be an inspiration. Becoming pain free is the goal and joy is the final destination.

"May you allow the destination of freedom inspire you to step forward."

Chapter 3
"Room For One"

Destination Solitude

This chapter is dedicated to isolation versus solitude. Personally, I was introduced to a combination of the two working in tandem at a very young age. Upon reflection, I have come to recognize that experience which lasted many years became the foundation later in life for me to navigate this component of my grief journey as a bereaved Mom.

When I was almost three years old there was a polio epidemic here in Nova Scotia and I was afflicted with that disease. For the next twelve years of my life, I was either in hospital, in the operating room, or laying on the couch at home or in my bed. Attending school was an off and on experience. My social life was very limited. There were no team or sport activities. My parents were exceptional in supporting me through those years and I shall be for ever grateful to them for making the difficult decisions that afforded me mobility in my life as opposed to being wheelchair bound.

I was someone who, for the most part, spent my time alone with my thoughts and my view of the world and those in it without much interaction with anyone outside the family. I am grateful for those years and the wisdom they imparted when I was so very young. I am happy to report that through the years the wisdom has far outweighed all that I have come to learn from others that I missed.

Let us explore the trap of isolation that makes itself so very available to bereaved parents and which we can easily fall into during our grief journey. We can keep company with isolation more than once and so can everyone else.

Keep company with is a rather ironic use of words when we consider the definitions of isolation which is the act of separating self from others, or solitude according to Mr. Webster.

I find the meaning between those two definitions to be quite different. One is voluntary and the other is involuntary. For me

personally, solitude is the outcome manifested when I choose to be alone for the sake of peace, serenity, and have time for thinking. It is a positive and healthy choice form of isolation and serves as a temporary reprieve from which we voluntarily return to rejoin the fold and our world. Solitude is in direct opposition to the other definition. The involuntary isolation form of separating self from others does not allow for any of the benefits solitude provides.

As a polio survivor, I would waffle between the two. The isolation was forced upon me through no fault of anyone really. It was the residual effect of my physical condition which put me in a place where I was separated from others. At the same time, though, I was fortunate to be able to experience solitude. I was provided peace and lots of time for thinking and observing. Though I experienced both I did not have the option of selecting one over the other. As bereaved parents, the good news is we are fortunate to have that choice.

Bereaved parents can get caught up in the isolation trap more than once while on the grief journey. I can affirm from personal experience that going there is not a conscious decision. This chapter will provide to you clarification around what catches us unaware, the why, and our response to it.

"A special message for Moms and Dads"

The involuntary form of isolation can present itself to us disguised as the path of least resistance. When we are alone or choose to be as it provides an opportunity to expend no energy, it can feel so appealing to us as bereaved Moms and Dads. Isolation wants us to believe it is a quiet and embracing cocoon-like place that will aid in our moving forward; however, in truth it is the place that will do just the opposite. It will behave like a spider's web and keep us stuck. There is no escape as is the case with solitude. It absolutely catches us unaware and feels welcoming to us.

There is no time frame attached to our isolation trap and it seems to arrive at those times when we are not wanting to feel. Feeling is the sense we often look to shut down when we are in pain and ironically is the one that was never designed for shut down. When those feelings emerge, consciously make the decision to opt for solitude and do not be afraid to reach out to others. Simply share with them the difference between isolation and solitude and where you do and do not want to be. Let them know how difficult it can be for you to be on the right side of these two entities and ask them for their support. They will be there for you. No man is an island and no woman is either.

It is critical we honour our feelings and not abandon them. To do that we also have to honour the internal driver we are blessed with upon coming into the world. Whatever name you wish to attach to your driver is fine; heart, soul, spirit. We must let the driver do its job as feeling is essential to healing our pain. Expecting to do that in the early days, though, can be too much to bear so be easy on you.

Feelings can be masked or temporarily ignored; however, they will always rebound stronger than ever. They are festering while not being given the needed attention. I can guarantee they are going nowhere until we are ready to face them.

When the time comes to face them, I would suggest you do not try to go around them and do not try to climb over them. We tend to resist going through them as it is a dark and painful path; however, going through them is a must. When considering the depth of the pain associated with our loss that we are forced to sit in, let me say that as scary as going though them may be, it is survivable and doing so brings light to your life once again.

Full exclusion is the only provision of isolation and goes against the rules of nature. When we are in isolation mode there is

absolutely zero percent chance of accomplishing any forward motion. Our potential cannot be accessed in isolation.

Involuntary isolation is a very unhealthy room for one and I wanted to share this piece of the journey with you because sometimes just becoming aware of its existence will perhaps have you avoid it or allow you to recognize what you are caught up in when it appears looking to claim you.

I would urge you to remain aware of the power of words. How we use them can be the difference between progress or not and can do much to improve communication between everyone.

"I choose solitude, not isolation."

Simply saying those words may keep you out of the room for one and the tangled web is brings. Please know you are never alone and always be open to reaching out. I cannot stress enough the importance of staying connected to each other.

"May you allow the destination of solitude inspire you to step forward."

Chapter 4
"The Hidden Self"

Destination Illumination

The instant we are made aware of our child's death is the exact same instant we are no longer who we were prior to the devastating event.

Before Erin's death I was a married woman with two beautiful little girls and we all enjoyed a home filled with much love, joy, hustle and bustle, along with a healthy dose of busy chaos. Working outside the home was an extension of me and all I was capable of and doing so allowed myself to be seen as more than Mom by the girls. I had spent many years working with the Royal Canadian Mounted Police in a public service capacity and loved every moment of that career. I had started it upon graduating high school at the tender age of 17. That twelve year tenure taught me much and built an awareness for me of all I was competent enough to efficiently master. When I found out Erin was dead, all of me was out the window. It felt as though the earth had opened up and swallowed me whole into a very dark place where I could not identify anything I was once so proud of and loved about myself. I had become totally consumed by the devastation that had been showered upon me.

I was not consciously aware of the above until after we had completed the multitude of decisions that must be faced in those early days following the death of our child. The notifications to family members and others, attending to whether organ donation is an option, waiting on autopsy to be completed perhaps, making funeral and visitation arrangements, and all of those thank you notes are the required actions by us. We are too busy with those decisions to consider anything else. As well the execution of those tasks can be longer for some depending upon extenuating circumstances that may surround a death.

It was following those early busy days, though, when everyone else who had been so attentive stepped back out and returned to their lives that I consciously discovered I had become a stranger to me. I remember sitting at my desk one evening pouring over all the beautiful expressions of condolences, donations and so on that had been made in Erin's memory with tears rolling down my face. Out of the blue I became aware of the fact that I had become a stranger to me. I remember jumping up suddenly and saying to my husband that my education and life experiences had not prepared me for what I was sitting in and feeling and asking how was I going to manage it all. He had no answers for me. He was struggling with as much pain as the rest of us. I did not like it and certainly did not want to accept this stranger. Many years of struggle ensued for me in this regard. Coming to the awareness I would never return to who I used to be and surrendering to that truth was not easy. I did not want to change as I had been happy with myself and my life.

Understanding the change is forced upon us and here to stay can be a challenge to us and others as well. It is particularly scary for us as the fear of the unknown surfaces. Our future self, our future life, and our future family are all nondescript. Everything has changed in a heartbeat and feeling at risk is an honest and not unexpected response. This distressing truth tends to bring anger right along with it and can create an additional burden.

There are a couple of analogies around what a bereaved parent really looks like and they will illustrate what we may see when we look at self. What we see is a reflection of what we are feeling on the inside and is very different from what others are subjected to when they look at us.

I would encourage you to become familiar with these analogies and this part of our grief process. After doing so, let me say that no matter which analogy speaks to any person more clearly, I trust

you may develop a sense of and truly see the great divide that has taken up residence inside a bereaved parent.

Having everyone be aware of and sensitive to this component of our grief journey is a gift as it can take years for us to plow through this one. Should anyone still need to know why it might take years if the great divide analogies described below do not click for you is to have you consider how many memories you have created during your lifetime with one of your children or another loved one.

Kindly recognize that when a child dies, the memories do not leave with them. They stay with the bereaved parents and now every single one of them is painful. To get to the place where Mom and Dad are able to control and remember them, and remember what they choose to without pain; along with making the many decisions about other aspects of their life in order to heal the great divide is a huge undertaking. We must all be patient.

"A special message for Moms and Dads"

An illustration of how this hidden self can appear and feel to us would be for me to have you imagine an upright standing and empty Egyptian tomb. The closed back of the tomb could represent what life looked like before the death of our child. The open front door of the tomb could represent what life will be like at the end of our journey; bright, exposed, reconnected to the outside world and feeling strong. Currently, you may be experiencing what is between front and back when the door is shut. Emptiness. We can feel suspended between the two. It is dark, confining, lonely, confusing and offers nowhere to turn.

Another analogy would be for you to imagine a tree being split in half, from top to bottom, with each half hanging onto the root by a thread. One of the leaning halves represents our life before and the other half represents the new life and new you we must learn to

accept and reach. Once again we are suspended in that empty space between the two halves.

It is my wish that sharing those analogies help to create for everyone some perspective of this great divide we did not ask for and for which we have had no preparation. We have been separated from what was, have no idea what will be looks like, and have no idea how to get there. We are literally hidden and stuck between the two. A component of our journey we approach with much uncertainty.

Working through that darkness to open the tomb's door to light or restoring the top to bottom split is not an overnight job. It can take years. We are faced with all kinds of decisions about what parts of our previous self and life we are going to bring forward and what parts we are going to leave behind. The art of letting go is a process all on its own. Many decisions will need to be made and they are not easy ones.

Identifying and acknowledging that I was now a stranger to me was a component of my grief journey I tried to resist for a very long time. It is a huge truth when revealed and not one easy to accept. The first step for me was only becoming able to admit I was a stranger to me. I had no idea what to do with it. The feelings of inadequacy, frustration, and anger that accompanied this element of the journey were monumental. The acceptance of this truth is a step forward but does not feel like it at the time.

May this information accelerate your level of knowledge as to why perhaps you are not moving forward as quickly as you would like. Our ability to move forward is enhanced as we deal with the many components of our grief journey. Always remember it is a piece meal process.

"May you allow the destination of illumination inspire you to step forward."

Chapter 5
"World of Weeping"

Destination Fearless Tears

My perspective on crying changed dramatically after Erin's death. May what I share here assist everyone in understanding this component of the journey.

I am a bereaved Mom who did not experience tears from the moment of Erin's death. Upon reflection, I see that I allowed my anger, my need for finding out what happened, and an attitude of having to take care of business so to speak become the drivers for my behaviours in those early days. I also now recognize that those drivers were being used to block the tears. I am probably not the only bereaved parent who has done that. The sadness was so deep yet not being expressed the way it should have been. Some call this denial. Maybe so. It is what it is.

There are three kinds of tears and the one that bereaved parents experience are called emotional tears and humans are the only members of the animal kingdom who have them. Our emotional tears are triggered when our feelings are heightened and they serve as a cathartic release in alleviating tension. That would explain why even though they may leave us feeling exhausted after the fact, they also can help us feel better. Emotional tears contain more natural painkillers than the basal or reflex tears. Women cry sixty percent more than men. Perhaps it is because emotional tears can also make us feel more vulnerable and often that comes more easily to women than men.

The tears were not at bay for long though and I have come to learn they have a job to do and it is our job to allow them to do it. Once those early days were taken care of and completed and I was within the four walls of our home they burst inside me like a hurricane. They came at that time when I identified I was a stranger to me and showed up without warning. I could wake up crying, go to sleep crying, cry while driving, have them fall into something I was cooking and not even notice until after the fact. They were in charge.

I was fortunate one day to be made aware of a beautiful yet bittersweet story. I am trusting the story will help others as it did me. The story allowed me to change my perspective just enough to make progress with all the tears and that is my wish for all the bereaved Moms and Dads in the world. Picture the following if you will.

Our loved ones are in heaven with all the angels where everyone is singing and each carrying a lit candle. One child's candle was not lit and the angel wanted to know why and the little one shared that it had been but that every time she lit it, her Mom or Dad would put it out with their tears.

Erin loved candles and singing. When I read this story it helped me immensely during those times when the tears I was shedding seemed too much to endure. It allowed me to regain some kind of control over how I managed them. I would simply visualize her happy, singing, and holding her 'lit' candle and wipe my tears away. Then I would force myself to smile. Doing so made me feel as though I was paying homage to her and keeping her light alive from a distance. Then I would look into a mirror and watch the smile that in the beginning I had to force but which over time became the welcomed natural response.

Should you be attempting to support and provide comfort to a bereaved someone who just can't seem to stop crying and whose unexplained tears show up without any notice whatsoever, arm yourself up with the information shared in this chapter and use it in your efforts. Sharing that little story could make all the difference to a grieving soul, no matter the loss.

"A special message for Moms and Dads"

I can still vividly recall those very tearful times even after these forty years. All those times when I didn't even feel tears coming;

however, there they were. They arrived out of the blue in total control and with absolutely no regard to where or when. This piece of the journey begins immediately when we allow it and can last more than a few weeks or months, even years.

To this day I value the gift of what I like to refer to as my fearless tears which came to me through this component of my grief. I have come to love and understand them. My tears now do many things depending upon the circumstances. I comfortably shed them when I am sad, happy, and sometimes they can even make me feel beautiful. I have been able to learn to embrace their purpose and they have more than one. I always feel better after I cry no matter the reason. I used to see them as a sign of me feeling weak but now they are a source and sign of strength and healing for me.

I can cry whenever my heart tells me that is what needs to happen and can do so with humble pride and no embarrassment. My hope is to never become so numb that my tears are no longer able to fall. In my mind, there is no gender protocol around tears. We are all supposed to use them and let them do their job of bringing us comfort. My heart controls my tears now and my brain is no longer in charge of them.

Here is a cute story I was reminded of while reflecting on this part of the journey. It is a fond memory which always brings a smile to my face. Enjoy it and may it make you smile also.

Erin's last Christmas gift to my Mom was a pair of Christmas candles which my Mom still puts out every year. When Erin delivered the gift to her, she said "Gramie, you will love these. They smell beautiful but will get very hot so be careful."

"May you allow the destination of fearless tears inspire you to step forward."

Chapter 6
"Fact and Fantasy"

Destination Truth

Bereaved parents experience hits upon the death of their child that are always accompanied by corresponding myths maintained by society. Addressing those, in my view, is a prerequisite to clearing a path for both grievers and non-grievers. In many facets of our grief journey truth and fantasy keep company and can create much conflict for both sides. Here is a fine example.

In those early days following Erin's death, I was quickly reminded of words and teachings I had received from the time I was very young. Such things as children are their parents' immortality, their legacy, and are meant to outlive Mom and Dad. Those beliefs were promoted within the home, within the church, in educational settings and certainly by society. After Erin was no longer with us, the aha moment for me was in recalling those teachings, I realized all of it was a myth and no longer my truth.

To have a child die before us is a complete reversal of nature and the cycle of life as we believe it to be in the human spectrum. This hit provided a harsh reality to that deeply rooted core belief instilled in me that I was supposed to die first and be survived by my children. That belief which was now uprooted wreaked havoc that went far beyond its surface meaning. This was a huge and difficult component of my grief journey for me and it stung far worse than any kind of sting you can imagine for a very long time.

My child is not supposed to die before me are words usually afforded lots of introspection and have been spoken by me and to me by every bereaved parent I have ever met or interacted with and that is a huge number.

The recognition of this new reality by me brought with it a myriad of feelings and emotions that required much fragmenting in order to navigate this piece of the journey. I found it to be confusing and often felt misunderstood when I would try to explain it to others. Looking back, I know now that I did not have the clarity needed to build my path through this one. Clarity revealed itself over time

and the steps to aid in your way out of this one are shared below. Until that happened, though, I felt like a very fragile bubble floating around and was unable to initiate anything. Surrounding the bubble was a big, dark cloud. Dealing with this lifelong core belief that had been shattered was a huge struggle.

Bereaved parents used to be like everyone else in our belief; however, we are no longer and that reality is one that has to be recognized and accepted by the outside world folks.

Therefore perhaps you can understand why when we hear the following comments we may not be receptive to them as they no longer fit what we are facing. They can be upsetting to us, puzzling, and create anger and sadness; however, quite often society expects us to respond with a thank you. That is difficult for us even though we know the intentions are good.

During conversations we may be told it was meant to be, it was God's will, it was time, he or she is at peace now and not suffering any longer. Such are standard messages of condolence we might receive as well.

More times than not, people looking to provide comfort to us walk away feeling as though they had not done enough or wished they had known what to say. Choosing to substitute the above comments with something like the following would benefit both sides. Of course, doing so would be subject to the circumstances and your relationship to the griever being conducive. This simple, priceless and true communication can be a gift to all.

Perhaps we could try asking Mom or Dad how they are managing having had their child die first because you know, we have all been taught that is not supposed to happen. Or maybe simply sharing that you are sure it must be very difficult having to face that reality.

Then sit quietly, listen intently, and ask for permission to feedback anything you would like to share once the griever has responded

to you. I know I would have appreciated someone having done that for me at the time.

Doing so opens the door for the Mom or Dad to share and feel safe to do so. This is a good example of how both sides can get comfortable with being uncomfortable.

"A special message for Moms and Dads"

Our child's death has exposed us to the myth of that core belief we have held our entire lives. Although taught to us by people who had the best intentions and with no disrespect to anyone, it was never true. Our reality proves otherwise and coming to terms with it can be overwhelming.

In order to manage this component of our grief journey, we are faced with a process that is difficult and time consuming. I am sharing a breakdown of the steps that worked for me as promised. Fragmenting the process can make it easier, however, choosing to do so is your call.

MY STEPS

I needed to question that lifelong belief.

I needed to let it go as it no longer applied.

I needed to identify and create a new core belief.

I needed to accept the new truth.

I needed to integrate the new belief into my life.

While coping with this process we are not able to give any thought to how those who taught us the original belief will manage this necessary shift we are forced to make. This component of the journey inflicts devastation that one who is not in our shoes cannot even imagine. It causes resistance, anger, requires much thought, and is exhausting as it is extremely labour-intensive.

The children are not supposed to die first core belief is deeply embedded inside our self. The readjustment takes time and when we are struggling with the shattering of the belief, comments shared by others which I have alluded to above can have little to no meaning for us. Even though we know they are being delivered with the best of intentions, know that they may not sit well with you and that is okay.

Along with processing this grief component comes the reminder once again that we are not in charge of anything except self. That reminder can bring to the fore thoughts of the protection and safety we provided for our children. Providing that came from our instinct. That permanent fixture inside self.

There is nothing unusual about reassuring our children they have nothing to fear. Mommy and Daddy would always promise to keep them safe, no matter what. We have all been there and done that. When a child dies we can feel as though someone or something has made a liar out of us. When we said that to our children, it was our certain truth; however, it can now feel far removed from our reality depending upon our circumstances.

We nurture, guide, love, and trust everything we have taught our children is sufficient to get them through life. We make sure they are out the door on time, that they eat properly, that they don't skip classes, etc. The foregoing leads us to believe we are in charge of all kinds of things and people. Some examples would be running a household, going to work, and providing for the family. We have

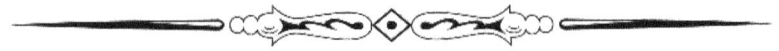

a responsibility to execute the above tasks while not really being in charge of any of them.

While considering that, facing the realization that you have lost the most valuable of everything, that one you loved so much, and the knowledge you could not keep them out of harm's way is devastating. Recognition of the no control is difficult and the acceptance of it takes much longer. When people think that what we are facing will never happen to them we must remind them that yes, it can happen to them. Another example of truth and fantasy.

The gift I received after working through this component of my grief journey was the creation and acceptance of my new belief "live in the moment as there are no guarantees of anything beyond the one we are in."

We could be compared to the story of the ugly duckling. We have to fight and claw our way into a new life that we want to love and be happy in, just as that little duckling did to return to the natural state of beauty we all deserve. We are faced with having to let go of not just our loved one, but tons of attachments as well. The reformatting process is huge.

> **"May you allow the destination of truth inspire you to step forward."**

Chapter 7
"Loss and Circumstance"

Destination Balance

Further to the previous chapter exploring my child is not supposed to die before me, it is important to look at a process I adopted in healing not only from the loss of Erin but the circumstances of her death as well.

Having worked for the Royal Canadian Mounted Police for many years and having had more than a few interactions with bereaved parents, I was no stranger to the protocol around losses associated with fatal motor vehicle accidents, suicides, homocides, sudden deaths, etc. I arrived home from the hospital the day Erin died fully expecting to receive a knock at the door some time during the evening and find a police officer standing there wanting to share with us what they knew so far surrounding Erin's death. I still only knew she was dead and that her schoolbus was involved. I was feeling anxious and apprehensive yet wanting at the same time to know more.

There were three knocks on the door that evening. The first one was a journalist from the local daily news whom I sent packing. The second was a beautiful lady who brought us food. A lady I had not met before but she appeared like an angel and was so very kind. The third was my caregiver who arrived much later as I had called her to come and stay with me as my husband was called away. No knock from the police though and a big red flag went up for me. Not even a telephone call. Both far removed from what normal police responses would and should be to a fatal accident.

The first thing I did the next morning after retrieving my car from work was go to the local Detachment to try and ascertain what was going on. I sat around a table armed up with a number of officers, some of whom I had worked with, and the man in charge of the Detachment, which caused another red flag for me. I was being treated as though I knew nothing about what they are responsible to do, was not supposed to be asking any questions and patronization was in full bloom and on display all around me. All I learned was that they didn't know anything yet. They had a question for

me though. What would I like them to do with her stuff? I got up, walked out of this room that was totally devoid of any respect for us or Erin with tears streaming down my face, got into my car and realized the circumstances were going to have to wait. They were simply too much to handle on top of the death itself.

Once I managed to heal the loss of Erin, I invested ten years in trying to get the answers to what had happened and it took me that long to connect with an officer who actually felt I had the right to ask the questions I was posing. He was willing to look into the matter for me and discovered why my questions were being ignored. No one had attended the accident and they had no answers as no one did their job that day. They did not even have her name on the accident report because they did not know who she was. She was listed as pedestrian. This aspect of Erin's death was a thorn in my side for a very long time; however, was healed once I took ownership of all I had done to right the wrongs and recognized that I had not failed, the system had.

No matter the age of the child, no matter the circumstances of the death; the pain and its depth felt by all bereaved parents is universal. However, it is important to be aware and sensitive to the circumstances which are often diverse and varying.

Accidental death, SIDS, homicide, suicide, at the hands of a drunk driver, stillbirth, miscarriage, casualty of war, and so on. I call these the death designs and each will require a particular grief design. Grief design refers to how the grief process will unfold and progress. Child loss creates a different reaction and healing path for each of us.

We should also not lose sight of the external factors that can contribute to the death designs. Examples would be bullying, cyber bullying, substance abuse, alcohol abuse, PTSD, anxiety and depression, illness, and so on.

The work facing the bereaved parent of a SIDS baby, for example, is not the same as the work facing the parent of a suicide victim. It is also important to recognize that even within a particular death design; for example, homicide, the processes can be wide and varied for the parents of those victims. All are individual and unique. The grief design process is complex within each individual category of death design.

Attempts by the bereaved to face and work through the death of the child and the circumstances at the same time can often reap no rewards. Be conscious of this point. Reading on will allow you to become familiar with the process I recommend to bereaved Moms and Dads. We often must work through the loss of our loved one first before attempting to come to terms with the circumstances. Trying to work through them together can be too much to bear and extremely exhausting.

I believe everyone should remain sensitive to and aware of the pain of others but not necessarily involve themselves in it.

"A special message for Moms and Dads"

Coming to terms with the reversal of the natural order when Erin died first put me in nightmare mode. I had been a once competent woman who could now no longer be in charge of anything. I was being controlled by my emotions and in public, I felt as though everyone else knew what had happened which caused me much discomfort. That included everyone I passed whether I knew them or not. It felt like I was outside of myself watching it all.

This normal state of grief made life difficult and being out of control of myself was enormously frustrating. I wanted to get back to me because I had liked who I was. Time passing revealed it was not going to happen though. Not now. Not ever. Child loss changes who you are. My little girl had died and I, too, was

nowhere to be found. Having to recreate myself and my world is what was awaiting me. I was years getting past this component of the journey.

Even while in our depths of despair, we should not forget that the same is no doubt true for each family member. They can also be struggling with a sense of losing self; albeit, to individual degrees. The process is uniquely personal and private depending upon the relationship and experiences they had with their loved one. Responses are varied and individual as well. Another component of our journey.

I was reminded through this loss of self that our development does not end with childhood. Just as children are a product of their environment we are for ever shaped by our circumstances. Any change in the dynamic of our environment causes changes for all those impacted.

A positive step in our process is to be cognizant of the behaviours you once had and the feelings and benefits they brought to you. For example, my behaviour of being in charge created a feeling of confidence for me and enabled a benefit of productivity.

Doing so reveals that it is not the behaviour that needs regaining. Rather, it is the feelings and benefits we enjoyed from the behaviour that we are truly missing. In my example, I was missing the confidence I had known. Once I had begun to focus on regaining my confidence instead of being in charge of me, I began to make progress.

I managed to make that shift because of my RCMP career experience wherein I would have to interact with people who had suddenly and tragically lost family members. Relative to those events, some of my responsibilities were administrative and others required me to deal face-to-face with the family members. The administrative responsibility was directly related to the

circumstances of the deaths; the face-to-face interactions were directly relative to the person lost. I kept those two areas of responsibility separate; so that how I approached the families was completely different from how I approached the administrative tasks involved with the same loss.

I feel fortunate to have been able to apply this same concept to my own situation and am so happy to be able to share it with you as it can be a huge aid in your move forward.

I separated the loss of Erin from the circumstances surrounding her death. In doing so, I acknowledged that the person lost challenged the responsibilities I had in my life; while the circumstances challenged my principles. Once I began to look at those two areas separately, I realized that my anger, bitterness, and all the negatives were related to the circumstances. An epiphany.

The benefit to separating the two is clarity. Clarity which allowed me to identify what required my immediate attention and to fragment what had happened. Instead of continually feeling overwhelmed by the stressors incurred with loss and circumstances combined, I focused first on healing from the loss of the person, Erin, and upon completion of that threw myself into coping with and working through the W-5 of it all; the who, what, where, when, and why.

Placing the circumstances and all they bring on the back burner for a time does not in any way negate their importance or impact. However, working through them with strength is critical and it simply isn't there for us in those early times.

"May you allow the destination of balance inspire you to step forward."

Chapter 8
"The Fragile Soul"

Destination Choice

Often while navigating and supporting the grief journey of bereaved parents, confusion and misunderstandings between everyone are manifested. They only occur due to a lack of communication, information, and courage.

It is important to share the feelings and behaviours grieving parents may experience and may demonstrate in the days, months, and even years after the death of their child. The feelings are the root cause of the behaviours we collectively can find distressing and are rightfully in full gear because a child has died. People can become witness to behaviours from the bereaved that are foreign to both the grievers and everyone else. These behaviours that will be expanded on throughout the book.

The list below is one to become cognizant of as it is representative of the root cause of the foreign behaviours. Bereaved parents are not always in charge of either the feelings or emotions listed. They control us for a time. Only the bereaved can determine the path and time frame attached to their grief journey. They are in charge of that yet may not be even able to address those two pieces until they have regained the strength to enable recreating self to the point of once again being in charge of the emotions.

Try to imagine yourself in that place and then validate what Mom and Dad are feeling. Let them know that whatever they feel is okay. This is invaluable. A subtle balance of understanding, knowledge, love and acceptance from both sides is imperative for everyone to be able to navigate the choppy waters of the delicate dilemma in front of us.

"A special message for Moms and Dads"

We may or may not verbalize to others what I am about to share. It may be some time before we can even clarify for self what we are feeling; let alone be able to admit it to self, express out loud, or

communicate to another. All are natural responses to the circumstances. Expect them. The list is comprised of my personal experiences as a bereaved Mom.

They may be part of what lays ahead of you; to be faced and worked through as you continue to step into this piece meal process of grief. Feel free to highlight any that you believe will be part of your journey. Should any of them create tears for you, take that as a sign it needs highlighting and attention as you continue to move forward.

MY I AM LIST

"I am sad."

The sadness that came to me upon Erin's death was immediate and unlike anything I had ever experienced before. I tried my best to push it away so that I could become somewhat functional; however, only to discover that doing so was going to be very short-lived as the sadness revealed itself to be a priority and I needed to pay attention.

Efforts to keep the sadness hidden from others in the outside world and in order to present myself as a somewhat functional human was exhausting and not productive or beneficial to anyone including myself. Ideas around navigating the sadness are scattered throughout the book.

"I am angry."

Anger showed itself to me on the very day of Erin's death and hung around for years. It has been my experience that the anger was directly related to the circumstances that led to her no longer being here. Initially I thought I was angry because she was gone but that was not really the case.

I was angry because for a very long time, years in fact, I was not privy to the information that would have provided me with a picture of what had actually happened as discussed in a previous chapter. I cannot stress enough the importance of separating those two entities, loss and circumstance.

"I am devastated."

Devastation permeated my whole being upon becoming aware of Erin's death. I had so adored her and all the dreams I had held for her and the ones we had shared in conversation had gone with her leaving me feeling so very empty and wondering what had been the point. Brutal realization was the unwanted gift of devastation.

I have had tons of losses in my life and without a doubt my child loss experience has been the most devastating of all. As previously mentioned it is a loss like no other and I believe it to be the greatest one.

"I am missing him/her."

Missing Erin was not anything I had to wait for as an awareness of that was immediate upon my return home from the hospital. Before Erin died, whenever I would come home from work, my husband and the girls would usually be hanging out, watching a movie or simply spending time together. As soon as I opened the door, I would hear Erin's little footsteps as she had always jumped up to run out and greet me. She would do that faithfully and with glee every single day. Run out to me with a huge grin and say "Hi Mommy! How was your day?" Without fail this was always my first gift upon arriving home and was followed up with my answer, my asking how her day went and a big hug between the two of us.

Arriving home that night and not having that happen reinforced for me how much I was missing her already and it brought forth anger and sadness. I recall seeing her Brownie book on the kitchen table which I immediately picked up and threw into the garbage while articulating that there was no longer a need for it.

There is so much being missed apart from the person that has died and it is a long term effort working through everything.

"I am lost."

For me I am lost was the feeling I had associated with wondering who am I, where am I, why am I in this place, and how will I manage this foreign territory. So much to consider so quickly. I was feeling totally disoriented, disengaged from everything and everyone and could not even begin to get past those thoughts.

This was a dark and lonely place filled with questions for which I had no answers. The answers eventually were uncovered as I traversed my journey and which you will come to know as you continue to move through this book.

"I am afraid."

One thing I learned while on this grief journey from a wise and well educated medical professional was that fear breeds anger. That made a lot of sense to me and gaining that knowledge was invaluable. It provided clarity relative to the anger element shared previously and helped me keep anger at bay when I was ready to step into the unknown that was facing me and of which I was so fearful.

Learning that fear breeds anger was worth its weight in gold as I was able to apply the benefit of that knowledge generously throughout my journey when anger showed itself and during those times when anger was part of the journey for other members of the family. It was at those times I would sit down and journal about what I was facing that was making me angry and ask myself what am I afraid of? Journaling the answers allowed me to be honest with myself and create a visual of what needed addressing. An undertaking I would recommend to anyone having the same struggle with anger.

Fear breeds anger was a huge gift and played an important role in the move forward.

"I am weary."

Weariness is one of our hurdles to overcome and can be experienced by the outside world folks as well. They can become weary waiting for us to move from the sadness or become weary of listening to everything. Weary sighs are not uncommon to any of us.

The weariness I experienced came from having such a full plate combined with the inability to think beyond the moment I was sitting in. That inability made all the moments the same and no decision making was taking place for a time.

"I am misunderstood."

Feeling misunderstood when I was experiencing the unrest Erin's death provided should not have surprised me but it did. Looking back I now know I was a stranger to me communicating to people who had known me for years but who were now also feeling like I was a stranger to them.

I was in foreign territory and the interactive nature of the relationships I had enjoyed with others before the tragedy was gone also and no dots were being connected when we were trying to communicate.

The communication breakdown is addressed more than once throughout these chapters as it is a huge component to be overcome by grievers and everyone else.

"I am broken."

For me being broken had to do with my heart. My heart felt like it had crashed and pained so deeply. At the same time, I recognized all the little threads of my life that had been attached to the heart felt as though they had been severed which perhaps was the reason my heart ached so much.

I really wasn't certain what any of it meant at the time or how I was going to mend it all. My personal story about my state of heart and feeling broken is the subject of the next chapter. Read on and become encouraged by the gift of transformation.

"I am confused."

There was no shortage of confusion when I was thrust into the role of bereaved Mom. I knew nothing about it. I had never been prepared for it and it was a polar opposite to all I had known up to the point of loss.

The confusion created much indecision for me. All of the components of the grief journey felt as though suspended in mid air just waiting for me to grab on to them, one at a time. None were identifiable, though, and I would not know what it was that I was going to be working through until I pulled it toward me. It was such an interesting process upon reflection because it turned

out in the end that as I had worked through each piece, they had come to me in exactly the order that eventually brought me back to joy. This surreal experience made me feel responsible for the actions yet at the same time confirming once again I was not in charge at all.

"I am stuck."

I recall what I mistakenly perceived as comfort during those times when I was in do nothing mode. Sleeping all the time, ignoring the outside world, not answering the telephone are all examples of feeling stuck. It was like trying to escape from being in quicksand. If I was quiet and unmoving I would still be stuck but I wouldn't be sinking further into it to where I might have to fight and struggle to survive it. Such is what feeling stuck was really all about. Not comfort at all

Many or all of the above are activated upon our child's death even when not recognized by us right away. Behaviours which are foreign to both us and others show up immediately.

The above feelings and emotions may not necessarily have always been part of your nature. If they were in the past, they are now enhanced. If not, they may be at play now. They tend to rear their ugly heads just as surely as the sun rises in the morning and sets at night. Emotions and feelings that we were once in charge of are now running the show. We do not have a choice and are hostage to them for a time. Validating their presence as well as their departure in time by you or others are both priceless gifts.

"May you allow the destination of choice inspire you to step forward."

Chapter 9
"State of Heart"

Destination Renewal

Our broken heart is usually accompanied by a broken spirit, a broken family, and perhaps even broken faith upon the death of our child. Everything is broken or so we believe. It sure feels that way.

As bereaved Moms and Dads we hold all the qualifications necessary to very easily become poster men and women for any advertising of a broken heart and spirit. We epitomize it. No one would use us for that, though, because it is not always visible to everyone. Not even to us. Our broken hearts cannot be viewed by any method; they can only be felt and we are the only ones who can feel them.

We could compare ourselves to those who have a heart condition requiring surgery or a heart transplant. The physically incapacitated heart can often be repaired; however, our emotionally incapacitated one cannot be helped by way of medical science. What we require is a heart transformation. We are the surgeon and patient all rolled up in one.

Sadly our broken heart cannot be mended; however, the good news is it can be transformed. My personal journey has taught me both those things and I am able to speak to both from that experience. I am very aware there are many, many bereaved parents who would disagree. Quite possibly the reason may be because they have not yet completed their journey. Perhaps they haven't even started it yet and are still attached to the myths, stigmas, and expectations of the outside world. Those can all play a convincing role in keeping us stuck for so very long. They did for me.

"A special message for Moms and Dads"

I have never experienced a heart attack which apparently is associated with severe pain. However, I believe the pain my heart endured after Erin's death far outweighed that of an actual heart attack. It lasted long after the event and impacted every single

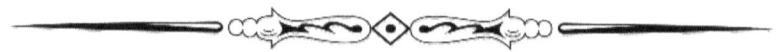

aspect of my life. It was when my heart was broken by Erin's death that I became very conscious of the heart purpose, apart from its physical one. As I alluded to in the previous chapter, perhaps the pain was so severe because all those pieces of my life that were attached to my heart felt as though they had been severed.

My broken heart transformation could be compared to that of a heart transplant recipient in that I did not end up with the heart I used to have but I did end up with one that works. It is one that allows me to experience joy and happiness; free of the pain. The new heart and spirit are ones that I have woven those pieces of me into that I love so much.

All of our traits and character qualities that we are blessed with and want to have as part of us are with us, for ever and always. My new heart is endowed with all I have learned about myself from my tragedy in combination with those pieces of the old me that I have always loved and chose to bring forward. So, in truth, my new heart turned out even better than the old one. I now enjoy a transformed and improved heart; one that is also available to each of you.

Like a surgeon, though, upon working to repair the deepest kind of wound; we are required to stitch, rearrange, and close the cut. We must do so while taking our time, being patient, and with courage. Also like a surgeon it needs to happen with the finest of precision. The band-aid solutions will not work, just as they would not work in a heart transplant.

Transforming the heart alters the life and vice versa. Sometimes one is the leader and sometimes it is the other. It is a roller-coaster, flip-flop, in and out of the dark tunnels kind of journey. It is not one that easily enables us to see with clarity any kind of progress. Having others watch, recognize, participate in and articulate the progress they see, though, is a gift to us. I have always believed that we should follow our heart long before we should ever follow

our brain. My life has been lived based on that philosophy. After all, the heart is the leader in the womb and deserves to hold that position throughout our life. We must honour the heart always.

The heart transformation is a process that is completed when all of the grief components have been taken care of and will be felt when the destination of joy has been reached. Look forward to and take solace in the knowledge that the recovery of a once again joyful heart is at hand.

"May you allow the destination of renewal inspire you to step forward."

Chapter 10
"Winds of Change"

Destination Courage

There is an old saying that has been around for as long as I can remember and it is very true. The only constant thing in life is change.

As a bereaved Mom my perspective has altered and I now know that in addition to the above, change often comes more easily when accompanied by its partner courage. One cannot be managed without the other.

We can all feel besieged by changes and challenges. They have a way of showing up when we least expect and often at the most inopportune times. It can especially feel so when anyone is going through grief and pain. Challenges typically bring change with them. They may be ones we are not happy with; however, there is no escaping these unavoidable aspects of life.

Coping with change and challenge for me includes an element of going to those places where time has a way of standing still and interacting with people who can offer up that feeling of time standing still. I find doing so creates a little balance in the midst of upheaval.

As a personal example I can share memories of visits to see my folks throughout my lifetime and which still hold true for me to this day as I am so fortunate to still have my Mom who lives life as a young 92 year old.

Visiting my folks, entering their home and receiving those hugs have always allowed me to enjoy that recognition of there being no time attached to touch. Those hugs that feel the same today as they did when I was a child. When I visit I allow the warmth of those hugs to wrap itself around me along with the warmth of the smiles, laughter, the baking smells that may be emanating from the oven, and something as simple as the cup into which Mom will pour my tea. The cup that has been in the cupboard for years just to be used by me. All are gifts of being in that place where time

stands still. It is an environment that has the ability to take me away from all the chaos and provide a reprieve for a time.

A trip to the ocean is another example for me of time standing still. The ocean and all it evokes in me never changes. It has a way of keeping me humble because when I stand in front of its grandeur, I realize how very insignificant I am. The ocean says to me I am valuable and at the same time, reminds me of where I fit in the big picture and allows me to humbly, yet proudly, maintain my place.

It is one thing to cope with a change that was initiated by self because we wanted it or needed it. It is totally opposite to be thrust into a change we never asked for or desired. Such is the case for bereaved parents. As I have mentioned before, we are put in a place of no knowledge, no education, no frame of experience and are all of a sudden expected to take on a role for which we have had no preparation. We have much to learn and much relearning to accept. Everyone should remain open to the learning for all to win.

"A special message for Moms and Dads"

I parallel the navigation of my grief journey to Erin's birth. As a first time Mother, I was learning as I went along upon her arrival and came to discover I was required to do the same upon her departure. It took courage to bathe and feed that little newborn, to nurture, guide, and love her. It also took courage to let her go, continue life without her and redesign myself and the life I was living. Please do not be too hard on yourself while on the journey and most especially in the beginning.

Connecting to my safe havens where time stands still assisted in holding me together while facing the changes and challenges. Doing so helped me to not give too much attention to the ticking clock of life. Experiencing that sense of timelessness served to

reduce the impact of the stressors the changes and challenges produced. Those safe havens came in handy both upon Erin's arrival and departure.

Time and timelessness keeping company has the appearance of a strange paradox and creates for me a rare glimpse into one of the many mysteries of life.

Search out your own personal safe havens where time stands still. Doing so and going there will be a wonderful support in navigating through the chaos and conflict.

Be innovative, be creative and be open to integrating all the positives that are available to you and throw everything into the mix with the negatives. Doing so will balance the scales and provide a better chance of weathering the storm and arriving back to joy and happiness as unscathed as possible. Positives and negatives can work well together more often than you may think.

When you are ready, willing, and able to create the changes you need and want in moving forward, that is your signal your courage has been activated.

"May you allow the destination of courage inspire you to step forward."

Chapter 11
"Starting From Scratch"

Destination Certainty

Life events can impact us in such a way that we are faced with whether there is a need to start over or start from scratch. Although the difference between the two may appear subtle, deeper inspection reveals how distinct they really are.

Some people think they both mean the same thing; however, I am not one of them. Starting over I have down to a science. Starting from scratch is a completely different process.

I have come to learn during my life that starting over is attached to the externals of life. Examples I could share would be that of having painted a room and when I was all done, I looked around and realized that no, this was not how I thought it would look. To repair that I only needed to pick another colour and repaint. Planting flowers that didn't take and having to replant is another example of one of my starting over experiences. These examples really didn't impact me too much on the inside other than perhaps feeling a sense of frustration. I only needed to make one decision. Was I going to redo or not?

On the other hand, any life event that does indeed jolt us internally is a starting from scratch one. There is no single decision with these ones. There are many decisions to be made.

Should you be someone who believes bereaved parents have to start over upon the death of our child, be assured that is not our path. It is important for you to be aware of this component as it will aid in narrowing the chasm between grievers and non-grievers.

As previously alluded to, my life's picture changed dramatically upon Erin's death. The internal jolt was huge and starting from scratch was revealed as the decision that needed to be accepted. . Whether that life picture change stems from child loss, spouse loss, job loss, or divorce they all require the same. A wiping clean of the slate, a reformat, rebuild and re-creation of self. By working through all the grief components shared in this book, letting go,

and accepting the new was my personal process. I made a promise to myself that I would find my way back to joy and committed to that promise. At the time I had no idea how that was going to happen; however, over time navigating this piece meal process revealed I just needed to be open to all that came my way and remain true to me. A labour intensive process but oh, so rewarding in the end. The death of my child turned out to be an end and a beginning.

"A special message for Moms and Dads"

Mom and Dad, our journey path is similar to baking a cake from scratch. We must carefully choose the proper ingredients, put them in their right order, combine them with care and love with the anticipation of a successful conclusion.

It can be overwhelming trying to identify the ingredients while in the midst of pain and sorrow.

There is no global recipe for our journey. There are as many recipes as there are bereaved folks. The ingredients are the same but the pattern is unique. How much of each ingredient we need to implement, when it needs to be added, and how it will be integrated are all factors closely associated to our loved one's death. Many variables abound.

A word of advice from me to you would be should someone say you will need to start over, kindly respond with no, actually I must start from scratch.

"May you allow the destination of certainty inspire you to step forward."

Chapter 12
"Here to There"

Destination Peace

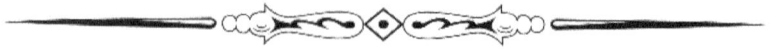

The grief process of a bereaved parent consists of a multitude of components that require shifts in perspective by us. This chapter is dedicated to looking at them individually as once identified on their own, it can be easier to fragment the process required to work through it.

Approaching the journey from that fragmented plan of action aids in avoiding the complexity that comes with feeling overwhelmed. The overwhelmed state only sets a precedent for accomplishing nothing. This act of fragmenting is difficult for the bereaved parent to even uncover, let along implement. An awareness by everyone can only serve as a positive impact all around. There will be many times when anyone may just want to give up or give in to the pain and perhaps knowing it is okay to break things down in order to work through them can serve more than once as a reminder to keep going.

This chapter will explore the shifts in perspective that bereaved Moms and Dads may need to master. Shifts shared below can often be resisted by us and upon completion by us, can often be resisted by everyone else. Change always requires the adaptation and acceptance by grievers and non-grievers.

These shifts in perspective could very easily benefit everyone, bereaved or not. I would encourage you to take a close look at the list as you might identify something you could apply to your life. Give some thought as to how any of them may positively impact any decisions, behaviours, or views you currently hold. The key difference in this aspect between you and the bereaved is the fact that you can make the shifts simply by deciding to do so. The process for us is more complex as the result of our inner storm which is expanded on in the next chapter.

Only each of you can decide whether you are going to hang around or not to support this piece of our journey. It is another labour intensive one requiring much time, energy and patience.

"A special message for Moms and Dads"

In our world of bereaved parental grief the shifts in perspective are necessary in order for us to restore happiness and recapture our joy of life. They are not shifts I recognized while on the journey. They are what I have come to learn upon its conclusion. In sharing that it is my hope that the information provided will serve you well. Welcome to the shifts I experienced and which I needed to fragment in order to move through them. Kindly adopt any that speak to you.

I HAD TO

Shift from all I had lost to all I discovered and had not known about myself.

Shift from the loss of my loved one to embracing the gifts she left behind.

Shift from pain and sorrow to the joy of life.

Shift from chaos and conflict to peace and serenity.

Shift from weariness to strength.

Shift from fear to courage.

Shift from couple disconnect to couple reconnect.

Shift from anger and regrets to forgiveness.

Shift from holding on to letting go.

Shift from dysfunctional to functional.

Shift from who I once was to my new transformed self.

Perhaps having a visual of my experiences will trigger something you can relate to and might be feeling. Hopefully having that will help lessen some of the confusion you may be facing. Also creating a list of your personal shifts required in your journal is a valuable undertaking with this component of the grief journey.

Each of the shifts shared that I had to make were individual journeys while at the same time were interwoven. These topics are all addressed throughout the book. There is no direct path for any one of them. They really cannot be approached one at a time to completion. They used to be connected for us but now they need reconnection. We could be likened to a strand of pearls; beautiful, connected and strong when intact but when damaged and broken require an investment of time and patience to rearrange, reconnect, and regain strength.

These shifts did not come easily or quickly for me; however, taking care of and recreating myself had to be first and foremost. I realized that only after that was achieved would I be of valuable service to family, friends, and the outside world in that order.

Doing so is not about being selfish or a me person. It is our reality. I will expand in the next chapter how to prepare yourself for these shifts, the steps to activating them and what that process will have you facing.

"May you allow the destination of peace inspire you to step forward."

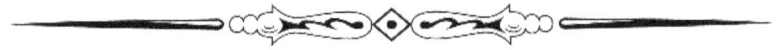

Chapter 13
"The Inner Storm"

Destination Change

Expansion of the information shared in the previous chapter continues here by taking a look at the inner storm that belongs to bereaved parents.

As mentioned each of the shifts in perspectives outlined previously may initially be resisted by Mom and Dad. This is especially true of those who were happy with who they once were and have not yet come to understand that there is no returning to it. Ironically, the piece we may not be able to acknowledge in those early times is the fact that the act of shifting will put us where we want to be and is what we are looking for. We just don't know it yet.

Upon personal reflection on all of my shifts I shared in the previous chapter, I am reminded of how many times I was required to move back and forth from one to another while enduring additional ones being revealed over time and added to the mix. One day would find me devoting time and effort into reconnecting with my husband to perhaps being distracted from that when the phone might ring and someone was looking for me to deal with an outstanding appointment Erin may have had scheduled from a provider who did not know she had been killed. I would explain that and once again find myself back in the doldrums causing me to feel any work I was doing on shifting from weariness to strength was a waste. Our journey is not really a two steps forward, one step back kind. It is more often a one step forward, two steps back kind.

We are similar to a soldier going off to war. The only difference being the war is at home and with self. Our courage may need rebuilding first as it is the main ingredient required to forge ahead with these shifts.

When you can develop a sense of our perspective of the inner storm described below and be accepting of it; such would be a huge gift to us. Especially in those early times of our bereavement.

Knowing the key challenges we face is one thing. How to work through them both individually and/or collectively is another and throughout this book, there will be expansions on these themes. Suggestions for all and alternatives to what you may currently be experiencing will be provided. I hope you will choose to adopt them when you feel it is appropriate to do so.

A lot comes up for us upon the death of our child and we are impacted by the outside world responses and behaviours; just as the outside world is impacted by ours. Both sides are in a state of confusion and misunderstanding; albeit temporary. I believe every person does the best they can with what they have to work with in any given moment in time. Should you be someone who agrees with that, then you would also have to agree that whatever any person bring to the table needs to be respected. Whether one is happy with it or not is irrelevant.

Harmony is not always at play; however, when one feels respected, the doors of communication open a little further. Mutual respect builds trust and high trust yields high communication. Such awareness allows for changes that will enable a peaceful accord to be part of the picture once again.

"A special message for Moms and Dads"

Along with now having been invaded by the unsolicited inner storm, we become the perfectly raging storm. Any emotions we would have been experiencing under normal circumstances that were positive are now negative ones. A few new ones have been added to the mix and our insides feel like a combination of tornado, earthquake, thunder and lightning, and any other storm of nature you can possibly imagine. They have all joined forces and decided to live inside us.

We want the storm to move on. We don't like it. It makes us sad and angry. It can paralyze us and keep us stuck. It makes us fearful. It may even cause us to become physically ill.

In nature all storms pass; however, not in the same time frame as in our circumstances. The external storms of nature pass much more quickly. While having the perfectly raging storm forced upon us, we are also the ones mandated to make decisions about how long the storm is going to visit, what path it will travel and when it will be over.

Please be kind to yourself and remember that figuring out how to do that when we are weary is often too difficult to think about, let alone execute. Know it will never happen in the time frame we would really love to experience. It is not a matter of us choosing not to move forward; it is more an issue of us not being ready, willing, and able to move forward. All three of those have to be in place first. Perhaps you are feeling willing but are not able or ready. Perhaps you are feeling able but not ready or willing. Perhaps you are feeling ready, but not willing or able. We don't intentionally stay in the storm phase because we like it. There is nothing to like and it holds no appeal. It may be all we can manage for a time though. That is okay.

TO ACTIVATE SHIFTS IN PERSPECTIVE

The first step is to acknowledge you have reached your enough is enough day.

The second step is to decide the storm has to go.

The third step is to harness that courage that enabled you to master the first two steps and decide to begin your work.

The fourth step is to refer to your journal and list the shifts in perspective you wish to focus on leaving enough space after each one to record your progress.

Healthy doses of time, energy, and patience are part of a successful conclusion.

"May you allow the destination of change inspire you to step forward."

Chapter 14
"The Eager Traps"

Destination Awareness

There are three traps which can put bereaved Moms and Dads in a quagmire. Traps that may not be typically evident to everyone else and create behaviours that are easily fallen into and may even be unbeknownst to the bereaved at the time.

Bereaved parents experience a myriad of new to us feelings and behaviours upon the death of our child. There are three, in particular, which are ignited and may show themselves from the early days of our grief and can last for some time. They are worthy of their own chapter and I consider them to be components of our grief journey that should not be ignored. Chances are you may or may not be exposed to them but it is critical to share them with everyone to provide an opportunity for others to have the necessary tools to support us in escaping the traps should we not be aware we have become victim to them.

One of the traps we can fall into can create a behaviour I refer to as expert procrastinator. I had never considered myself to be a procrastinator throughout my life. I was always one to jump in and get things done when they presented themselves. Perhaps that came from having been so removed from everything in those early years when I was coping with my polio needs. Later in life I was usually at my best when I had a neverending to do list. The more I had to do, the more productivity I enjoyed. Procrastination did not fail to escape me, though, in those early days following Erin's death. Do nothing mode had been activated along with any desire on my part for it to disappear for a time.

Please feel encouraged in the knowledge that it was temporary for me and I eventually reached my "enough is enough" day. I wish the same for all of you. One day I woke up and felt ready, willing, and able to move away from procrastination. As mentioned before, ready, willing, and able always need to be working in tandem in every component of our journey and this one is no exception.

Another trap we can fall into can create a behaviour I refer to as worry warrior. Again, this is an aspect we have to work through and often we do not see it right away. Therefore if it is addressed to us by you, it may not be received well. I would still encourage you to do so, though. Sometimes having our attention drawn to something can provide a much needed aha for us. Even if it is not received well at the time, the important part is done. The bottom line is you cared enough to share. What we may worry about and how we respond to it are expanded on below. This behaviour is fear based.

The last trap can create a behaviour I refer to as death wisher. It may not be what it seems on the surface; that being thoughts of suicide. Presumptive beliefs such as that one on the part of others can leave us in a place where we don't feel we can share our thoughts. Kindly embrace the information shared below for the grievers.

"A special message for Moms and Dads"

As mentioned before we bereaved Moms and Dads understand only too well how precious the gift of time is and being afforded the opportunity to wake up on any given day is a consciously recognized truth for us after our loss.

However, even with that knowledge, it is super easy for us to want to just go back to bed. Truth is, we may not have even managed to get out of it in the first place. Staying in bed, staying immersed in sleep should we be lucky enough to get some can engage us and hold much appeal. We can handle doing nothing beautifully and particularly love not having to face anyone; as alluded to when we looked at isolation.

That is what comes easily for us in those early days and months. It can be a monumental undertaking to take a shower, cook, appear presentable to others, and live life in general. The world at large

is still spinning around as usual and our little world is spinning as well in a much different way. Our spin is overwhelming.

This behaviour is one that can easily have us become a victim of the expert procrastinator trap when we are not careful.

Recognize this is all temporary; however, perhaps being aware and able to anticipate its arrival will prevent you from even going there. You are capable of staying out of this place. Just look at all you have done from the time your child passed until the point where you are home and everyone else has left. Many important decisions were made and executed. The visitations, funeral, notifications, and so much more. Give yourself credit for all you have managed while coping with your pain of child loss. There is no other loss like it. Nothing can compare.

Remaining mindful of those qualities you have that contributed to your successful handling of such decisions is critical. Remembering they are always accessible and utilizing them can keep or get you out of this trap is beneficial.

The death of our child has a way of immediately instilling a sense of doubt or fear and can put us in a state of worry. One of the most immediate worries we are forced to work though is the burial of our loved one, no matter their age. We do not want to let go of them. For some, there is not even a body to bury.

Another worry that surfaces can be manifested toward the surviving siblings of our loved one. Becoming over protective of them is as easy as slipping on a pair of shoes.

Whether or not we were someone who was that way before our tragedy, it will appear and can accelerate to proportions that will not serve anyone in a productive or positive manner. It can create rifts we really don't want or need. I have to say I feel most fortunate that I did not adopt this behaviour. Luckily the ramifications of becoming over protective surfaced for me and

prevented me from giving this behaviour any attention. I am not certain where that awareness came from; however, have felt blessed through the years to have had that happen for both myself and Heather.

Falling into the worry warrior trap and adopting this behaviour is based in fear. The thought of if it happened once, it can happen again kicks in. Such is our reality. Everyone loses when worry abounds.

The third behaviour is one that appears horrific and scary to the outside world; however, is one that best reflects the depth of our pain. Some Moms and Dads will express it to others while others will not. They will carry the thoughts inside and they can so heavily weigh on them. I call this trap death wisher when we are wishing we could die, wishing we were with our child, or not wanting to be here without them.

The thought of death can be appealing or so it may appear to us and others. Some would presume we were speaking of suicide; however, I don't believe that is what we are speaking or thinking of at all. That presumption by others can preclude us from sharing our thoughts as we do not believe they would understand. Having to do so can be likened to torture.

Every person in our life fills certain needs we have and their absence does not negate the needs still existing and requiring attention. It is my contention that when we utter or think those words above that appear to be a death wish; what we are truly feeling yet perhaps not recognizing is the feeling our needs are no longer going to be met because the one who met them for us is no longer here. The death wisher trap can be easily misconstrued by both grievers and non-grievers.

"May you allow the destination of awareness inspire you to step forward."

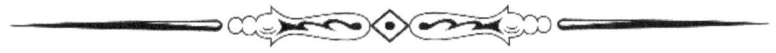

Chapter 15
"The Daily Struggles"

Destination Ease

People might be shocked to learn how the very seemingly inconsequential tasks of daily living can become major obstacles inside the home of a family who has had a child die. Another component in this piece meal journey we shall refer to as the nitty gritty of life is the topic for this chapter. Dealing with these tasks are emotionally taxing and can wreak havoc. They are ones rarely shared outside the four walls of the bereaved family home.

Asking us how we are managing the particular task once you are aware would be beneficial as, once again, we may not even be cognizant of the connection between the task and the distress it is causing as we may be in the throes of weariness, anger, and sadness.

"A special message for Moms and Dads"

The daily struggles posed some of my greatest difficulties in those early days and weeks following Erin's death. They were not ones I would ever discuss with others for fear they would appear mundane to anyone not in my circumstance. Nonetheless, chaos and conflict prevailed while creating mixed emotions.

As a wife and young working Mom of two girls when Erin was killed, there was never any end to the nitty gritty tasks facing me. All of a sudden what used to be labours of love had become burdens.

Being a family of four there was never a shortage of laundry to be done in our home. I will never forget that first load of laundry I went to work on following Erin's death where her belongings were still in the hamper. Taking her clothes and looking at every single piece and wondering what to do with them. Wash them, not wash them, throw them away, save them for Heather were all thoughts that came and went so quickly and offered no solution. All I could do was cry and angrily wonder how something so humdrum as laundry had become so tormenting.

Before Erin passed when doing laundry I used to think it would never end and often wished it was less labour intensive. Those thoughts came back to haunt me when I was faced with laundry waiting for me after Erin's death. All of a sudden it was less labour intensive and I felt bad for having had those very normal responses prior to her death because now I was wishing for all the laundry in the world if it would have meant her return to us.

Setting the table for dinner was another huge stumbling block for me. For many weeks after Erin passed I would grab four place settings from the cupboard and be reminded that I only needed three now as I proceeded to set the table. The sheer weight of carrying that fourth one back to the cupboard stays with me to this day. It always felt so much heavier than it truly was and this daily snag was exhausting and emotional.

Often I would not remember until I was going through the checkout at the grocery store that the summer sausage I had in my hand was no longer needed. I was purchasing it for Erin. Having to apologize to the cashier and returning the item to its shelf was painful and embarrassing.

I now know that if someone had told me to expect these challenges and the range of emotions evoked by the daily tasks at the time, I believe I would have responded to them differently. Certainly, the fatigue level would have been lowered.

It can make all the difference in the world when we are prepared for something to happen with the assurance that it is okay. Instead of beating myself up about those negative emotions I had, I would have recognized the daily task experiences were normal to the circumstance and temporary. Prior knowledge would have enabled me to look upon my struggles as progression rather than regression.

You may find it beneficial to journal a list of the daily struggles applicable to you and opposite each, write down and become aware of the emotions they evoked in you. Some of mine included anger, sadness, shame, frustration.

May this information be beneficial to you in working through this component of the grief journey.

"May you allow the destination of ease inspire you to step forward."

Chapter 16
"Timing the Aftermath"

Destination Thought

Following our child's death we are faced with many time sensitive decisions surrounding the funeral, visitations, burial and so on and when completed we exhale a big sigh and look forward to a reprieve of sorts. In short order, though, the myriad of decisions relative to round two show up and these are the ones that have everything to do with timing. They are not time sensitive yet can cause great strife and be quite troubling.

While we are contemplating these decisions, we are also faced with deciding when we are supposed to address them. Navigating these decisions to completion can keep us stuck for some time as it takes energy and thought when we are weary. Recall there are no rules of grief.

"A special message for Moms and Dads"

Once we are past the funeral and everyone who was by our side has gone back to their lives, we become very aware of life continuing to go on around us whether we are participating or not. However, we are left to engineer the solutions to the barrage of aftermath decisions that are often only known to us. We may share them with others. We may not.

I remember giving so much time and thought to deciding not only what to do with Erin's things and any changes to the bedroom she shared with Heather but when. Even though she was no longer with us, Erin surrounded us still. Each and every time I would come across something of hers, I was faced with a decision and those somethings were in every room. There was no escaping them. From small to big and anything in between had to be looked after. From the toothbrush in the bathroom to the bed she had crawled into every night. From the clothes in the closet and bureau to the toys and renderings on the fridge of her artistic endeavours.

Along with knowing decisions had to be made, I was filled with angst at the same time. I would often find myself in her room and

taking an item of her clothing to hug and smell while crying in an attempt to hold on to her. The decision about what to do with her clothes was one I delayed for a long time.

As for the bedroom, I made no changes there. I made the decision since the girls shared the room that it would probably be in Heather's best interests to not have too many changes at once. She had already shared with me when she learned of Erin's passing that not only was her sister gone, but her best friend as well. In those early days, I simply asked her if she was okay with their room as it was and she said yes. I told her that if and when she ever wanted to change anything to just let me know and we would take care of it. That decision actually was positive in that everything in their room could stay as was for a time and alleviated a few of the hurdles facing us. Everyone's input is so valuable and often has a gift or two attached.

Trying to figure out when we are supposed to return to work, get back to life and wondering if we will ever be happy again are all hurdles to be faced. Be reminded again, there are no rules of grief.

Should we share these decisions with family members, friends and others, they will have lots of suggestions regardless of whether we asked for feedback or not. Truth is, though, unless they have been where we are, they really don't know what is best for us. No matter how kindly or compassionate their intentions are, a clear understanding of what we are sitting in is absent for them. Only another bereaved Mom or Dad would be familiar and able to provide the voice of experience.

The solution that worked best for me in answer to all the decisions involved in this component of my grief journey is the same as always. When I was ready, willing, and able. In having remained consistent to that concept from 40 years ago to current day, I have learned and continue to implement what has become one of my greatest gifts of bereaved motherhood. The gift of having my

priorities straight and making decisions at the right time for the right reason. Doing so brings me joy just as not doing so brings no joy.

I simply gave myself the time I needed to think, stay in tune and true to my own inner self and allowed it to guide me in all these decisions. Adopting that concept allowed me to know when to make each one. Some decisions took days and some took weeks. Others took even longer. Whatever time you need is your call and is okay. Be selective when making your choices.

Using a journal is such a good habit to develop and can easily become a best friend. Making a list of the decisions facing you provides a great visual and moves it from your head to paper. In doing so you may find that most, if not all of them, will deal with items of an external nature. In other words, outside of self. Write about the impact your decisions have had on you.

After doing so and once you have rectified everything, consider whether your attitude changed with respect to the level of importance you once placed on the externals. Creating a new priority list will let you know what is now most important. A gift.

"May you allow the destination of thought inspire you to step forward."

Chapter 17
"The Family Connection"

Destination Knowledge

Regardless of the size of the family and the family loss, the impact of our child's death on each family member is significantly individual because each has had a unique relationship with the one no longer here. Another consideration needing attention is the pace at which each family member is able to grieve their loss. Grief pace and the individual feelings of loss within the family unit are differences that can have us believing we cannot help each other. We may not even be aware of what is going on for another family member.

Let me provide a personal shining example. May doing so help everyone in our efforts to move forward.

About a week after Erin had passed, her younger sister Heather came to me with a request. This was a four months shy of turning five little girl. It was evening and she asked me if I would turn out all the lights in the house and just sit on the sofa. I did as she asked and she knelt on the floor in front of me and told me she had something to say. I said that whatever she needed to say was okay and I just listened quietly. I made sure I was going to *hear* her. There is a vast difference between simply listening and actually hearing.

I later realized the darkness request allowed her to express herself without having to see what she feared the most; the possibility I would not *hear* her and the rejection that would have created for her. Remember, this was one suffering soul speaking to another suffering soul.

She told me we used to be a family of four but were now a family of three. She said one was missing and would never be back. She told me she still needed her Mommy and Daddy and asked if we were still going to be a family, just different. In that moment I saw this as a beautiful example of that well-worn phrase "out of the mouths of babes".

Heather's comments allowed me to identify that her sense of security in our family was threatened and she needed reassurance the family would remain intact for her. The benefit to me was huge. I had just received the gift of inspiration that would become a catalyst to my move forward. She had made me aware that in my suffering and not participating in our day to day care in those early times, I was, in fact, unconsciously contributing to her image of the shattered family which I did not even know she had.

My perspective was we were still a family; however, in her young and impressionable mind and heart, it had been threatened and was at risk of vanishing.

In that moment I became aware of the individual loss that exists. Not only had our family unit been altered encompassing all the things we had enjoyed as a group; there was also a yet to be determined impact on smaller pairings within that unit such as Mom and Erin, Dad and Erin, and Heather and Erin. Just as we each had shared certain pieces of self with Erin, so had she with each of us. Privately.

"A special message for Moms and Dads"

Realizing we cannot ever fully relate to the loss for another because we were not privy to those one-on-one encounters is a gift of valuable information. Each person has their own unique memories to deal with and need to deal with them in their own way and in their own space and time without interference. We can only support each other with those collective family experiences for which we have a frame of reference.

I cannot stress enough how beneficial it is to everyone when we truly *hear* the messages family members may attempt to convey. We can only try to relate as best we can. However, perhaps having this information can clear some of the fog that easily permeates

our home in those trying times. Sometimes just understanding why we may feel as though we aren't getting through to another can help make it bearable.

The ripple effect is diverse and far reaching because what I have shared is at play with anyone who ever interacted with your loved one.

This component is one for which using a journal is beneficial. Create a list of the names of people and their relationship to your child. This could include not just family but perhaps even friends of your loved one whom you may no longer see and who have stopped coming to visit. Beside their name create a list of the losses they are experiencing; including those you know about or ones they may choose to share. Asking them to contribute in this exercise can be very revealing. Either way you may discover things you did not previously know.

Sharing this component with others and gaining knowledge about what is missing for them serves as a powerful support in the efforts to maintain and enhance a fluent family connection.

"May you allow the destination of knowledge inspire you to step forward."

Chapter 18
"You Plus One"

Destination Respect

It is important to bring attention to bereaved Moms and Dads not as parents but as a couple. Whether your status is married, separated, common-law, single or divorced matters not. The two were a couple at some point or still are.

If, in sharing my personal experiences relative to this component of our grief, anything rings true for you, know you are not the only one to have ever felt this way.

Many things changed for us as a couple after Erin died. We had two very good longtime friends, a childless couple, who were like second parents to our girls. They were an enormous help during the visitations and the funeral and drove us everywhere. We wouldn't have made it without them. They drove us home from the funeral, and we did not see or hear from them ever again. Parents with whom we had socialized and whose children had been Erin's friends also disappeared. Our once potential support network outside of family began to dissolve. It sometimes felt like we had fallen off the face of the earth.

We knew they weren't being intentionally hurtful. It was about them not being comfortable with the loss and not knowing what to say or do. Everyone is in pain and struggling. Hopefully this aspect has improved over the years.

Other losses we experienced as a couple included the usual life events. Going for coffee, chatting about what to get for groceries, preparing for holidays; to name a few. Our one to one connections as a couple were disappearing and try as we might, we were unable to recover them. Nothing seemed to have the importance it once did for us. All felt lost.

The most difficult piece for us as a couple had everything to do with how each of us chose to cope with and respond to our loss and the ensuing stages of grief. We selected very opposite paths.

I felt the need to get books, read, and try to understand the process in front of me. I had never been down this road before and knew I had to educate myself. My husband just shut down emotionally. He would continually tell me he was grieving in his own way. There is no doubt men and women grieve differently. My husband had also fallen prey to our generation's belief that men are to be strong for everyone else. I trust that myth has been debunked. For us, the day Erin died, so did my husband in a lot of respects. At least that was my perception.

Recall what I mentioned before about family members grieving in conflicting ways and at varying speeds. This was most apparent in the couple connection for us. The connection which became our increased disconnection as time passed. One of us had made the decision to move through the grief process and the other had not. When we were immersed in this period of our lives, we did not see it for what it was.

"A special message for Moms and Dads"

Throughout these past forty years since Erin's death my interactions with other bereaved parents have been plentiful including a few where the child's death was one that perhaps had blame attached to it that was being carried by the Mom or Dad. I cannot even imagine how difficult that aspect of a circumstance must be to work through. I have always felt blessed to have not had to face that additional hurdle and I have the greatest respect for those who overcome the challenges that circumstance presents.

Research has revealed that the separation and divorce rate among bereaved parents was extremely high in the 1980s and I believe that may still be true. It took me seventeen years to recognize that in 1984 I had subconsciously decided to not ever be included in that group. Though, in 2002, my husband and I did end up parting ways after twenty-nine years of marriage and having had two more

children. Many years later my ex-husband shared that the accident had shattered his confidence in life. Wow, what a journey that would have been to try and come through. Such was a reminder to me, once again, that we each do the best we can with what we have to work with in every given moment in time.

The success you may experience as a couple is not for me to predict. One thing for sure is to recognize the couple connection /disconnection is an ongoing work in progress which requires time, patience, and equal effort and commitment. In our case we are no longer together; however, are still good friends and always will be. A gift we cherish. A bereaved couple who manage to reinstate the couple connection and remain together have my utmost respect. Kudos to you.

Creating a list of your couple disconnections you have had even if you are still no longer together can be helpful in moving forward. It is important to identify what has been lost and what needs you had that it filled. What you used to have in your life as a couple is a missing element that through time needs to be either replaced or recovered. An integral part of the rebuild.

"May you allow the destination of respect inspire you to step forward."

Chapter 19
"Integration Not Closure"

Destination Strength

I sincerely trust you can take what I share and apply it to your circumstances in a way that will support you in moving from sorrow to joy. That is my wish for you.

You will often hear people say that bereaved Moms and Dads need closure. That is what society as a whole believes. Bereaved folks come to learn over time there is no such thing as closure and it pains us to hear others use that word. What we need and must do in order to move closer to joy is something called integration.

Closure is defined as bringing an unpleasant situation to an end so that you are able to start new activities. Closure does not apply to the bereaved family because our situation is not just unpleasant. It is devastating. We are way past unpleasant. Starting new activities holds no appeal for us when we are grieving. We are in foreign territory and we are fearful of the new as it is unknown.

On the other hand, integration is defined as the process of combining two or more things into one. Please be reminded of the analogies I shared previously about the Egyptian tomb and split tree. Those visuals represent what we are sitting in and everyone should be understanding of that and recognize them as the beginning of our path to integration.

I am reminded once again and amazed by the value of the perceptions and input from Heather were to our healing process at such a tender age. This memory is a clear illustration of the topic at hand.

A beautiful Nova Scotia gal you may have heard of by the name of Anne Murray had a collection of songs for children in the marketplace in the 80's and I had purchased it for us. The girls loved all the songs and we would enjoy a concert from them every night before they went to bed. Their renditions of those songs were a blessing to us. Erin would perform some, Heather would perform

others and then there were the duet ones. The singing and dancing was very dramatic and entertaining. Joys to behold.

When Erin was no longer with us I often gave silent reflection to those concerts and wondered if Heather would ever want to rekindle that piece of her life. What I would do if she did was a struggle to come to terms with and I decided it would come to me at the time. Sure enough, she came to me about a month after Erin had passed and asked if we were still going to have concerts. I told her if that was something she still wanted to do she could. At the same time I was thinking to myself how painful is would be for each of us as suffering was still very much a part of our lives.

We restarted the concerts under Heather's terms which were in the dark and with her curled up under the desk and that was okay. Doing so was an eye opening revelation that yes, we will never completely close the door to the past and yes, we will integrate parts of the past into the now and future.

It is so strange that we are encouraged to carry the events from our life with us as we grow and age; however, when a child dies, we are encouraged to put it behind us or get over it and seek something called closure from those who have never been where we are.

"A special message for Moms and Dads"

Heather taught us the importance of integration. The taking of what was part of the person we have lost and including it once again into our lives. She helped teach us that doing so is okay. It returned some joy to us although a different brand of joy for everyone which was okay. After all doing so is what our loved one would have wanted. Over time the lights came back on and the dancing resumed.

I would encourage you to journal a list of events in the realm of daily fun and family times that stopped upon your child's death and give some thought as to how you can integrate them back into your life. Those memories are part of your life experience and you cannot leave them behind. You must carry them forward and use them always.

The topic of our precious memories we worry so much about losing will be expanded on in the next chapter.

"May you allow the destination of strength inspire you to step forward."

Chapter 20
"The Essential Memories"

Destination Comfort

Over time bereaved Moms and Dads become aware of the many components of letting go attached to the grief journey. One of them which can be most difficult is called memories. Memories are defined as the recalling of people, experiences, and information.

This chapter is dedicated to those memories that can plague us and the ones we fondly remember. They all have the power to aid in our move forward.

Memories we hold of our child can show themselves in many forms. They may be the ones we carry around privately inside of self. They may be the ones reflected in all the external things and belongings accumulated throughout their life. They may be the ones which are often revealed to us when in the company of others who recall times they spent with us and our loved one. Some of those may be brand new to us as perhaps have never been shared before. Just sitting in the environment in which our child resided will elicit tons of memories.

"A special message for Moms and Dads"

We may be exposed to two challenges regarding our memories. The first is the fact that no matter their origin our memories have a way of flooding back to us in an instant while working through our grief. They are back on the scene when they choose and often not at the most opportune times. Having them do that can be burdensome.

I can remember expressing that perhaps we should move to another house as the one we were living in presented memories at every turn and in every moment. That was very wearisome, and my sadness and anger prevailed. I thought moving might get me to the place where I could once again be in charge of what memories I wanted to conjure up and when. Researching that decision revealed that after a tragedy such as child loss, no move is recommended until after at least two years have passed.

While recognizing we will always want to recall them on our terms; at the same time we may be fearful they will leave us over time. I can confirm that the memories do tend to fade in and out while on our journey; however, when you are done you will identify they are still intact, clear and bright once again and available to be accessed by you when you choose. They are our remember when memories and a gift restored.

In our second challenge we may be faced with the fear of possible loss of the memories impairing our ability to begin our letting go aspect of our journey. Worry about that can play a part in our timing of the aftermath tasks; for example, what to do with our child's room, things, and so on. Let's expand on that one decision all on its own because it is so very tough. I have learned that letting go of possessions does not negate or void the ownership we have of the memories they conjure up for us. There is nothing wrong with letting go of the external possessions which no longer serve a useful purpose in the life you are sitting in now. Only to be done, though, when you have made the decision that you are ready, willing, and able. The remember when memory will still exist. It is not connected to the possession, it resides inside you.

When our child has died, much conflict, chaos, anger and dysfunction can occur for our family and extended family; especially when approaching family gatherings and special occasions. They can put us in if only mode and it is easy to stay stuck there.

In approaching those events, it would not be unexpected for us to think about if only our child were here to participate or if only it was their turn to have the special event. All of those things we were robbed of are what comprise our if only thoughts. If only there was a graduation, a wedding and so on. Then there is the most painful one of all, if only we could have seen our tragedy coming.

I vividly recall the evening of the day Erin died when I laid on our couch. I was utterly devastated and just wanted to be alone with

my swirling thoughts. I did not yet know the details of her death. I only knew she was gone and it had involved a school bus.

As I had laid there recalling the time I had with Erin I realized that if I could have been given the opportunity to have her back for those six short years I would not have changed a thing. It was in that moment that I made the decision to get myself through by recalling only the remember when and not even go to that place of if only.

The if only serves to fuel where we do not really want or need to be. If only has no purpose other than to keep us stuck. What we did not and will not get to experience has no role in our re-creation process we find ourselves in as bereaved parents. Focusing on the if only make us feel worse and simply adds more stress.

The flip side to if only is remember when. Which reminds me of a remember when story I would like to share.

When Erin died we had a cat named Rags. She was an orphan cat who just showed up at the door one day and we adopted her. Erin loved her very much. Often at times when I returned home from work, tired and began making dinner, Rags would get underfoot and I would snap at her to stay out of my way. One evening, Erin looked up at me with those big baby blues and reminded me that Rags was just a cat who did not know she was bothering me. She shared that the cat was not smart like people and that I should be kinder.

The gift I received from that remember when story was one of awareness. Erin reminded me of a basic piece of information that I already knew but was forgotten in the hustle and bustle of daily life. The lesson was patience and respect for all things which has stayed with me on a much more conscious level through the following years. I treasure and value this gift from my little one.

We experience wonders almost every day yet we often do not consciously acknowledge them or see them. When we take the time to stay in remember when mode, over time we come to recognize the gifts we received attached to those times. The gifts that were given and the lessons that were taught to us by our special someone and others. The remember when has a way of bringing a smile to our face and creates thankfulness.

I feel fortunate to have not had regrets during the time I had my Erin. Perhaps that was because she was here for such a short time. Should you have regrets, do not beat yourself up. Simply recognizing that you might change something if you had another chance is a gift and a lesson. Treasure that knowledge.

When you choose to give yourself permission to recognize your remember when gifts and lessons, you have moved yourself closer to then being able to verbalize them to others. In doing so, you are then relaying a subtle message to others that they, too, are allowed to speak of the experiences they had with your loved one. It also helps to fill that need we have to hear our loved one's name being spoken by others.

You will have removed the fear that exists for people who really would love to speak up and share their memories. The purpose of memories is to be a source of comfort and they will do just that. To journal your memories, good or bad, is beneficial. I cannot stress often enough how valuable visuals are in supporting the move forward and clearing space for the new in front of you.

"May you allow the destination of comfort inspire you to step forward."

Chapter 21
"House of Loyalty"

Destination Honour

Another component to our grief journey that deserves attention is something called loyalty. Loyalty is often looked upon as the allegiance or commitment to others and to undertakings.

After having travelled my bereaved Mom path, I have personally amended that definition to include self. Loyalty for me is now the allegiance or commitment to others, to undertakings, and to self. Another gift gleaned from the tragedy that stays with me to this day.

Where we place our loyalty is something we should all give thought to on a regular basis, bereaved or not. Taking stock of who we may have in our lives who exhibit true loyalty is as critical as maintaining distance from those who do not. The comments in this chapter are specific to the bereaved.

I would encourage everyone to give some thought to the following question and become clear about the answer that applies to you and your situation. "Where is my loyalty being housed?" It is important to gauge this piece while on the grief journey. Also, take a moment and ask yourself "To whom or what am I dedicating my precious precious time and energy?" These questions are great ones to journal about and I would recommend doing so for clarity's sake. I love the value of pro and con lists as they are great aids in decision making. For example what are the pros and cons of devotion to self as opposed to devotion to others at this time in your life? Food for thought.

What others may often perceive as a selfish behaviour on the part of bereaved parents is indeed necessary as described below. Becoming familiar with this aspect of the grief journey being faced can improve communication when awareness exists for both sides.

"A special message for Moms and Dads"

For bereaved parents including the word precious above is of the utmost importance because we have been forced into acknowledging in a heartbeat the fragility of time and energy. Ours is particularly precious because we are faced with a lot of down time during our grief journey and are no longer recipients of the 24/7 productivity choice. What used to be the 24/7 available to us can be reduced to any number from 0/7 to 24/7 on any given day and there is not a thing we can do about it. Therefore we should pay close attention to what we are doing with our limited and valuable up time.

It is our own self that the down time is serving and our up time should be as well though perhaps not always the case. It requires a conscious decision by us to do so. Loyalty to self is key in our efforts to navigate the journey. **To do so is not selfish. It is necessary.** Being clear about our loyalty to self is required for us to figure out how we are going to get comfortable with what we are sitting in first. Only then would we be able to explain our circumstance/feelings to another and have them actually get it. To believe otherwise is unrealistic.

Here are some suggestions I would encourage you to consider and perhaps adopt in your efforts to become clear on your loyalty status. The choice is yours and only you can decide. These are some ways you can be loyal to you and they will assist in returning you to a joyful state.

Recognize and live in the moment as it may be all you can manage.

Allow the tears to flow as they are in charge for some time.

Remain medication free when you can. Medication only serves to waste time in escaping the inevitable.

Have someone to talk and vent to who simply listens and make it clear that is all you need from them at that time.

Get hugs daily even if you have to hug you. Emotional well-being requires a minimum of four per day.

Allow music, fresh air, and nature into your life every single day.

Attempt to journal once a day. Writing about thoughts and feelings will clear space inside of you and make room for the new.

Bear in mind that each of the foregoing will be implemented only when you are ready, willing, and able and you will know when the time is right. The timing for each can vary. Until you do, you are really not able to care for others in the way you might like to without feeling burdened by the effort. Be totally devoted to you for a time at least.

Loyalty cannot be bought. It must be earned and our circumstances have provided that to us along with the need to be committed and loyal to self. Loving self enough to become the best you can be only ends up bringing the best you have to offer to others. That is worth waiting for by them. Patience by all is key.

"May you allow the destination of honour inspire you to step forward."

Chapter 22
"The New Normal"

Destination Power

In navigating this grief journey I would be remiss to not address the component that relates to truths and misconceptions. They are active in our grief and impact both us and others.

This chapter is dedicated to sharing a truth about normal that can surface for bereaved parents upon the death of their child. Normal can be defined as a usual or typical condition causing one to conform to a standard. Also it can mean to do what is expected. The truth we once held prior to the death was that normal existed for self and others. After our loss our reality changed to no longer having a normal while at the same time others were still living theirs.

What is often considered to be societal protocol is in direct opposition to what would be realistic expectations for bereaved parents. Exploring truths that immediately appear upon the death of a child for us in conjunction with the expectations society seems to hold will reveal another gap and opportunity to close the chasm I mention between the grievers and everyone else. Bear in mind truths we feel may not be ones we are able to articulate right away.

We eventually get to the place where we are living to the beat of our own drum and anyone, bereaved or not, who lives that way already understands the concept. To ask a bereaved parent to return to normal by society's definition and expect that we will is purely an illusion. It will never happen. Attempts to do so are time and energy wasters for both sides. This kind of discussion creates only aggravation for all concerned.

"A special message for Moms and Dads"

My bereaved parent role allowed me to see how commonplace the outside world expectations of normal were while I was sitting in a place where mine had been taken in a flash. While existing in foreign territory after Erin's death I was made very aware of the expectations from those outside my world. My optimism

witnessed by others throughout my life was now pessimism and my openness to discussing anything with others in a non-judgmental manner over the years had now become contemptuous. These changes in my behaviour were used as opportunities by others to place labels on me. Others felt they had the right to do so because they knew me, or so they thought.

We get bombarded by all kinds of influences assuring us that we need to return to normal. Upon completion of my grief journey, I now know that to be an unrealistic and impossible request and we should not ever give it any consideration. We cannot acquiesce to it because we are faced with recreating everything. Recreating self, then our life with family and friends, and then the outside world in that order is my suggestion. Doing so is a gigantic undertaking and one not always realized by us in short order.

We are forced to undertake that process to the beat of our own drum. Circumstances require us to dig deep inside self to utilize all that is there to move us out of the depths of despair and into our new life. When we get there we see we have created a new normal that is unlike anything we had before and one that works well.

Prior to our journey as a bereaved Mom or Dad our definition of normal was typically the one society as a whole projected and considered the acceptable meaning as shared above.

As you travel your journey and bring it to completion you may discover your new normal will be defined in a way that will see you gifted with the ability to continue on to the beat of your own drum. You may come to learn that you have developed a normal defined as the adherence of expectations you have set resulting from a standard created by you and to which you can easily conform. Such has been my experience and gift. Embrace the power that comes with living life marching to the beat of your own drum.

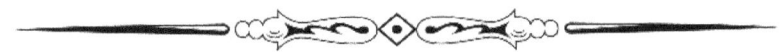

"May you allow the destination of power inspire you to step forward."

Chapter 23
"Unknown to All"

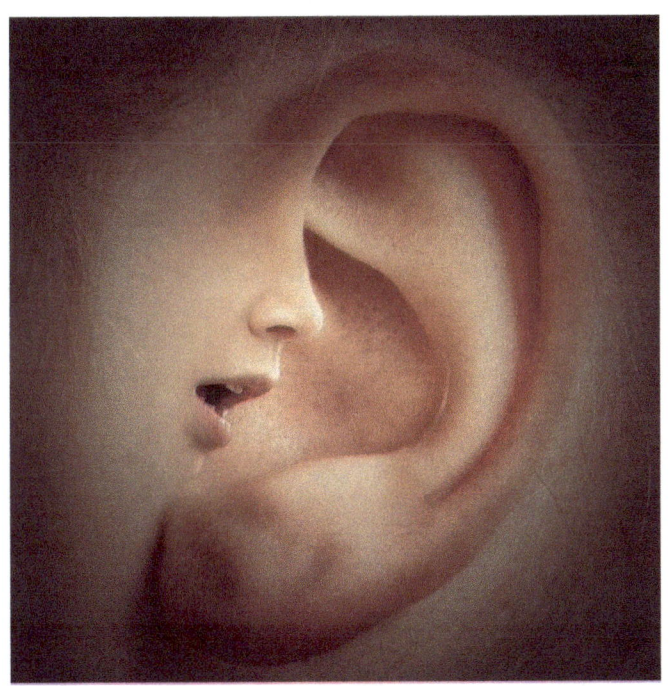

Destination Reconnection

In expanding on the previous chapter, let us have a look at another of the truth and misconception scenarios that surface for bereaved parents.

A truth we held before our loss was that not only did others know us, we knew us. The reality after the loss for everyone is no one knows us now.

What has become the truth for the bereaved is the recognition of loss of self. The harsh and factual new truth to be reckoned with by everyone is quite simple. We are gone. We are no longer the person we were and never will be again. There is no going back as everything has been altered. As immediate as that recognition is for the bereaved, it is a reality not often accepted by the outside world folks. You are not alone with that, though. It is not a reality we are very accepting of either as it is not anything we want to acknowledge, let alone attempt to work through.

We understand you may be wanting us to move forward and get back to our old selves; however, it is simply not available. In time, we will have recreated ourselves to a point where pieces of who we were are integrated into this new world and this new me but until then, you and the bereaved are strangers.

"A special message for Moms and Dads"

As is mentioned more than once throughout this book, how others used to communicate with us no longer works because we are no longer who we once were. A change in the approach from others is a required element in order to enact a restart to the communication breakdown that now exists. This non-negotiable change and acceptance applies to everyone.

Coming to terms with this component of our journey requires much time and patience and is a rocky road. We may not

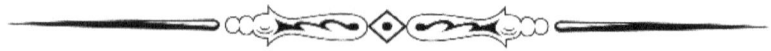

understand it and we certainly don't want to be accepting of it but we must and will be eventually. It is a critical ingredient on our path to joy. Perhaps by my sharing this knowledge and experience I have had, you will receive a lessening of the conflicts that we are often faced with from others who do not have a frame of reference for our circumstance.

Over time as your journey progresses and after much integration and healing you will no longer be strangers with the outside world folks. You may find both sides, having become open and aware of the existing circumstances, are armed up and both are now able to forge and restore relationships even better than what was once enjoyed. Another gift of grief.

Whenever you are feeling up to it, I would encourage you to share any information in this book that is applicable to you with the outside world folks. Only you can explain what is going on for you with any credibility. That ability may not happen for you until the journey is over and if that is the case, no problem.

Breakdown in communication exists in many components of our grief journey and it will be mentioned more than once throughout the book. Regaining the communication element is an ongoing process while travelling from sorrow to joy. Be patient with each other, listen to each other, and then hear each other. Slow but steady will eventually win over this obstacle filled course.

> **"May you allow the destination of reconnection inspire you to step forward."**

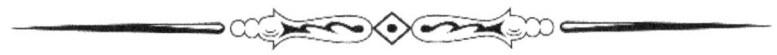

Chapter 24
"Tale of Woe"

Destination Trust

In this third truth and misconception scenario example, we are faced with having to endure something that may require us to go against one of our core principles. An ugly and exhausting necessity for a time that can take a huge toll on bereaved Moms and Dads.

"How are you" are three of the easiest and most common words we ask another person. It is a natural and normal question. It flows off our lips perhaps even more often than those other three words, I love you. Then there are those three words most of us respond with under normal circumstances. People will answer with "I am fine". Bereaved parents may answer with I am fine after the loss; however, that is a lie. Our reality is something quite different.

Even under normal circumstances when no tragedy has occurred, I would suggest it is a small percentage of the population who are really asking how another is doing from the standpoint of sincere interest as opposed to simply being cordial and the same would apply to those answering. I am fine is the easy way out and prevents us from having to share something that perhaps we find embarrassing or keeps us from having to take time to spend time with each other.

Before asking how are you to bereaved parents, I would encourage everyone to give some thought to why you are doing so. Consider whether it is simply a matter of being cordial or whether you have a real and heartfelt interest in the response. Should the question be one of normal cordiality only, please understand we may be forced to lie. Real and heartfelt interest could be expressed in another way and may enable us to speak truth.

Offering a simple hello, it is nice to see you, or it is great to see you out and about can take the pressure off us. When it is heartfelt, express that truth. Suggestions such as getting together and having a chat, coffee, are all positives for us. Letting us know that you would really love to know how we are getting along or not and

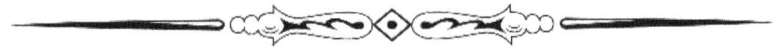

wanting to know what you might be able to do to support us would be music to our ears.

We may or may not be in tune with the outside world and making such efforts provides us with something different to think about for a change. Others taking on the role of initiator creates a win-win for both sides.

"A special message for Moms and Dads"

Managing how are you can be one of the most debilitating aspects of our journey. Even though responding with fine or I am fine might appear to be the easiest route in the moment; truth is doing so can create a lot of conflict for us. Both responses are lies. Lying causes us much pain and takes a lot of energy; however, we simply don't have the level of energy that would be required for the truth. Not only are we not able to be honest with others due to concerns that come up for us if we did, we are not being honest with our own self either. Such is the plight facing us.

It can be exhausting trying to determine who really wants to know the answer. A concern for us is why do they want to know. Will anything I share remain with them or will it be shared elsewhere by them? Such are examples of concerns we can experience and not always consciously and questions for which we need honest answers.

When the outside world can adopt the suggestions outlined above and you are coming to understand that you may be facing a person who is genuine and heartfelt in their communication it helps to alleviate those concerns we have and at the same time gives you permission to share them. In doing so, they can be eradicated for your interaction with the special person who truly cares.

When both grievers and non-grievers are ready, willing, and able to exchange truths from a foundation of mutual trust, exposure to another one of the many lifetime gifts of grief is unwrapped.

"May you allow the destination of trust inspire you to step forward."

Chapter 25
"The Quick Fix"

Destination Worth

This chapter is designed to provide an option for the bereaved to adopt a truth philosophy that may help to catapult them over the "how are you" hurdle specific to the outside world folks who only ask out of perceived cordiality.

As an expansion to the previous chapter in which initiation by the outside world was encouraged; it is equally important to enable an initiation role on the part of the bereaved. When both sides are open to initiating, progress is activated for a successful conclusion to this journey to joy for everyone.

My experiences of stepping back out into the world after my loss was a component of the journey that became an education onto itself. Not only did I feel vexed by "how are you" and "how are you doing" as alluded to in the previous chapter, I was equally vexed by those comments I experienced the most. The nothing at all ones.

It was not unusual after Erin's death to see people I had known for year often bow their heads as they passed, look away or pretend they did not see me at all. Some were people I had previously worked with for years.

It was hurtful and I felt the rejection. Reflecting upon those times, I came to realize the reactions of others were really coming from a place of ignorance and discomfort, not malice. At some level I did recognize that their heart was with me, regardless.

"A special message for Moms and Dads"

As bereaved parents, it is important to recognize others often have no frame of reference from which to draw that could provide them with any knowledge of our nightmare.

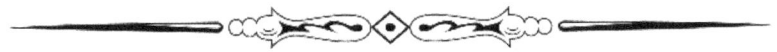

I learned that it was up to me to set the stage for a reconnect. I did not wish to invest any longer what little energy I had in responding to the question with "I am fine, thanks" and moving on. That was not my truth and it pained me to lie. I was tired of doing so; therefore, I created the following for those who did choose to speak. I trust the time will come for each of you to utilize the following as well with the wish it works for you like it did for me.

They would ask how are you and I would attempt a smile if I was able to manage one and share my truth philosophy. I would very kindly share that I was having an honesty day and that should they really want to know how I was doing I would be happy to share. Then without taking a pause would continue with the option that if they really didn't want to know that was okay too. They just needed to let me know and shared that if they didn't believe they were ready or could cope with my truth, that was not a problem either. I encourage you to give it a try.

Setting it up for others and letting them know that whatever worked for them was fine with me gave them permission to share their honest thoughts. No longer did they feel they had to say what they thought was best for me. Doing so revealed their true motive. Interestingly, most people really did want to know. Often people just don't know what to say or do.

Should you be approached by others during those times when you are having a bad day but still need to be out in the world, feel free to honestly share that today is not a good day, please forgive me. Maybe we can chat later if you would like to get together and thanking someone for asking, letting them know you appreciate the effort are huge benefits to both sides. Simply communicate truth.

Those little honesty day spiels can work wonders. It brings smiles and joy as it allows everyone to be genuine. A very freeing experience which often provides the bonus of hugs.

Now for those others who did not have the courage to speak or look at me; I just left them alone until I was strong enough to make the first move. When I did, I was able to reconnect with them also. The piece I had to be sensitive to with this group was the recognition that the more time that had elapsed when there was no communication, the more difficult it became for them to do so because perhaps feelings of guilt or shame were permeating their being; further preventing them from approaching me. In time I took on that task of reconnecting with them and it always ended very positively.

Eventually, they would share their reasons for having avoided me. They told me about their discomfort, how they did not know what to say and how that made them feel. Looking at them and letting them know I understood and validating their feelings can be a source of joy for everyone.

Such conversations provide an opportunity to educate those folks on how they may choose to handle similar situations in the future. My initiating the reconnect contributed to easing their pain and helped me with mine as well. We both ended up being better equipped to face the grief of bereaved parents we may be required to interact with in the future. In the midst of grief, I had not only moved myself forward but someone else as well by reaching out. That is a powerful experience and one I believe we can never have too much of in this world.

Our re-entry to the outside world is a component which is a beneficial one to journal. I would encourage writing about your experiences once you have stepped back out. What has been said to you? Who is avoiding you? How have you responded? Reflect upon how much truth is really exchanged.

Once you have identified the answers to those questions, pay attention to the feelings evoked in you during and after the interactions. List them in your journal.

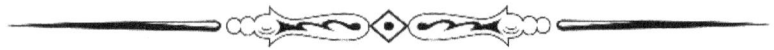

One gift attached to this component of our journey is recognition and appreciation that losing my child has put me in a place whereby I no longer expend energy wasting time. Those phrases, however cliché they might be; the truth hurts and the truth will set you free have proven themselves again and again to be invaluable stimulants in my grief process.

Personally my sensitivity to and compassion for others at a time when I was suffering has become a huge part of my recreated self and it is another gift. I love it and I believe you will also. I have been for ever grateful to have discovered that my considerate side could have been elevated to heights I never imagined. I wish the same for each of you. Everyone is worthy of being treated like a priceless gem and speaking truth brings merit to all.

"May you allow the destination of worth inspire you to step forward."

Chapter 26
"The Pet Peeves"

Destination Relief

Bereaved parents have a lot of what I lovingly refer to as pet peeves with the outside world. As well, the outside world have their pet peeves with us. To maintain a level playing field this chapter will explore both sides and what is going on for each. This is a component of our journey which can be a huge contributor to the communication breakdown between everyone. Exhaustion and annoyance is all around.

I remember a lot of time being spent pondering these questions that came to the forefront for me. They came up in the early days and extended far into my grief journey.

Where are the people I used to always be able to count on?

Why are those people I have known for years avoiding us?

I noticed that those who were keeping company with us were not speaking Erin's name and when we did say her name, they appeared discomforted and seemed to find it depressing.

Why did the people who had never lost a child think they knew what was best for us?

Why didn't others feel we should honour our child on special occasions?

These are just a few of the pet peeves this bereaved Mom experienced and which were usually unasked to others by me.

Emotions evoked by these thoughts for me ranged from sad disappointment to angry frustration.

The pet peeves of the outside world folks can look something like this and may very well be unasked to us by them also.

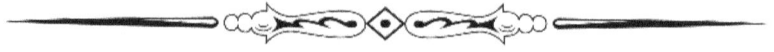

Why won't we stop crying?

Why won't we stop staying in bed?

Why haven't we gone back to work yet?

Why are we not heeding any of their suggestions?

Why can't I get through to them?

Wondering about why Mom and Dad are not closing the book and getting over it is often a mystery to the outside world folks. I would suspect the emotions evoked for the outside world folks are very similar to the ones I experienced.

Silence is not always golden. Everything both sides are experiencing is the same and a diverse collection of factors are contributing. Fear, discomfort, a feeling of being ill-equipped to cope with the situation, sadness, anger, misconceptions, and judgments may be running rampant. We are all facing a big ball of confusion that needs to be unravelled. We may be feeling as though we are darned if we do and darned if we don't. The good news is it can be remedied over time.

"A special message for Moms and Dads"

Truth and honesty are the first steps to reconciling these issues. The pet peeves on both sides are reflective of the concerns everyone has and as heart driven as they are, none of them will take any of us to where we need or want to be. Both sides have a

role and responsibility in the communication vein as it applies to this component of our grief journey. It still needs to be a two way street yet so very different for each side. We must all be prepared to put aside the fears and worries that may preclude us from speaking our individual truth. Both sides must also be prepared to hear what is being said and receive it without judgment. Simply expressing to another your inclination to adhere to both those suggestions can open the door and clear the path to remedy the pet peeves and can perhaps result in an even more improved common ground than what previously existed. As mentioned before, fears and worries will fall to the wayside when the desire for the outcome being sought becomes greater than the fear itself.

We should never forget how critical it is that everyone remain cognizant of the knowledge that the old communication style no longer applies. Life has changed dramatically and resistance all around can be a given. Reminders of that will show up intermittently throughout the book as it is so very important.

We must also realize that others are doing what they think is best, along with what is best for them. Others may not be conscious of that and we should always maintain an awareness of it. Typically we are not open to suggestions made by those who have never been where we are. We must be willing to share honestly with them our new reality in order to help them understand what we are in and facing.

We are the experts and as the old saying goes if you are not part of the solution, you are part of the problem. I fully understand, as should you, that it may take years for you to get to that place. It did me.

Sharing both sides of our grief in this book is meant to accelerate the process for all.

"May you allow the destination of relief inspire you to step forward."

Chapter 27
"The Gossip Mill"

Destination Resolve

As we are all very aware, the gossip mill has been around since the dawn of time and is not going anywhere anytime soon. Its sole purpose is to elicit not so positive behaviours from the mill members and bereaved parents, more often than not, are negatively impacted by them.

Actions and behaviours are what they are. They can be good, bad, and ugly. We each make our own decisions and the ramifications of such are the sole burden of each of us to bear. No one is responsible to take on those of another.

In adjusting to the death of our child, another component we must face has to do with our own personal truth questions. Becoming familiar with some of them may give pause to anyone who opts to be an active member of the gossip mill. It is my wish these questions will move people from perpetrator of rumours to supporters of truth.

Often kept to self, bereaved folks may struggle with not only trying to figure out what happened to their child; we wonder how it could have happened and was there anything we could have done to prevent it.

Here in Nova Scotia back in 1984, Erin's death was blamed on a blind spot that apparently existed as our busses were not equipped with bubble mirrors. A brochure that would have only cost ten cents to produce explaining the existence of the blind spot to parents would perhaps have saved her life but there was no such brochure and no one knew about the blind spot except the system and the drivers prior to her accident. I had a very difficult time dealing with the belief I had held that every morning I was handing her over to someone who would take care of her. Never for a second did I doubt her safety. However, truth is she was not safe. She died at the hands of her driver. I had taught Erin to always stop at the centre line and make sure oncoming traffic was stopping before crossing all the way and that is exactly where she

was upon first being struck by the bus. The driver failed to wait for her to cross and obviously did not check for her to have done so before proceeding as is required by law.

No one participating in the gossip mill were privy to any of the foregoing information; therefore, none of that truth was being shared. It was years after the fact before I gleaned the truth myself.

We may question our parenting and ask self if we are being punished. We wonder if perhaps we could have done more for our child. We think about how good a person our child was which conjures up all that we loved about them and which will be missed for ever. No one knows our child like we do which gives only us the right and privilege to speak real and authentic truths about them, about what happened to them, and about the relationship we had; whether good, bad, or anything in between.

These are just a few of our truth questions and the answers are not always pretty. They will be addressed by the bereaved over time, when ready, willing, and able are in tandem.

These truth questions are the justification and stigma fodder for others and can keep the gossip mill spinning for a very long time.

The marks of reproach, shame that is created for us and our loved one, and feelings of being disgraced are experiences showered upon us; thanks to the members of the gossip mill. Not only is information being shared that may not have been obtained from a first-hand knowledge source; it is often shared by people we don't even know and yet what they say is actually given credence. Grain of salt tales abound.

Read on to gain some perspective as to what should really be happening for and by both sides.

"A special message for Moms and Dads"

The truth questions do not belong to anyone but us and the same applies to the answers. We are the ones who have been given the designation and responsibility to address them. We are burdened by the questions and the effort it is going to take for us to put them all to rest. We own it, to be faced and dealt with by us, and only us, on our terms. There is no compromising with this component of the journey. The feedback from the gossip mill always reaches us and only adds to the burden.

You have earned in most devastating fashion the right to stand your ground and let another know that until permission has been granted, no one else has the right or privilege to share what isn't theirs to share. It can be so exhausting trying to dispel the rumours of the gossip mill. We need only concern ourselves with our truth when it comes to this part of the journey. Everything else is irrelevant and only zaps what little energy we have.

When the gossip mill is in full swing, the scales are tipped and only the mill members can balance them. No one needs or deserves to be either a victim or a perpetrator.

"May you allow the destination of resolve inspire you to step forward."

Chapter 28
"Engineering the Path"

Destination Leader

Everything in life is a process and grief is no exception. Our grief journey deserves the same respect and attention we might give to anything else.

The time always arrives when bereaved folks need to reckon with what path they are on and decide whether they want to stay there, shift gears and move into a different one or simply stay stuck by just not giving it any thought at all. These options are not specific to bereaved folks as anyone could apply the same concepts to most aspects of their life at any time.

In the case of bereaved parents, the decision is theirs to make although it is my hope someone would always be watching so that should a hurting someone choose a path that is detrimental, intervention is available. I do not see grief and bereavement as mental health issues although they are often pushed into that category. However, I will add that like anything else that is not without exception. Grief and bereavement are emotional issues and normal responses to losses endured in this circle of life.

"A special message for Moms and Dads"

Another gift I have gained from my grief as a bereaved Mom relative to this component of the journey is the knowledge that when I chose to not go with the flow, I created my own. The same one I have to this day and which continues to serve me well.

I was a number of months, if not more than a couple of years following Erin's death before I had accumulated enough information from my grief experience to attempt the move from my deep despair. However, my enough is enough day appeared and it was decision time. I had been stuck in my grief long enough to recognize it was not the place where I wanted to live out the rest of my life; therefore, staying stuck in it was no longer an option. I still had a husband and a daughter who needed me and they were

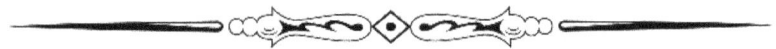

a source of inspiration to motivate me into forward motion. I told myself I was ready, willing, and able and that I had the courage to make it happen.

Believing in myself enough to make the decision to move forward and return to a place of joy in the knowledge it would be done my way was the first step to creating my own flow. Positive outcomes do not stem from having confidence; they actually stem from believing in self. Self-belief breeds confidence.

Our own flow, once revealed, will show the way and when it does deserves to be trusted. As I have mentioned before every person's journey is unique. It is travelled in one's own time and space. It is no other than the one which works for you. Everyone has the right to exercise their own flow without having to feel badly about it or having to explain it to anyone in order to receive acceptance. Only you can be your own best leader. We and others have an obligation to ensure it is not detrimental to self whether grieving or not.

It is critical to not fall into the trap of waiting until we feel up to it to make the decision as that day may never come. We must at least be willing to do our best to search out and identify the catalyst that will jump start the path forward.

How we behave, how we choose to embrace our life and pain following a tragedy has a direct impact on those around us, just as we are impacted by the same from others. We can choose to forge ahead and stand strong in the face of adversity or sit in it for undetermined time frames. This is the case no matter the loss. There are varying depths of adversity; however, no one holds a cornerstone on pain. No matter the age of our child or circumstances surrounding their death, the pain experienced by all Moms and Dads is universal. Only the approaches to it differ.

Often we will hear bereaved folks say "I feel numb". When I hear that what comes to mind for me is no, numb is an outcome we experience in difficult times. Putting it out there as a feeling, though, can create confusion. The correct expression would be "I am numb". Numb will dissipate when we trail back to what needs our attention, meaning the cause, and making the decision to begin the repair.

Though the destination I wish for all of you is happiness and joy, the path though the pain for each is different. We are each our own engineer. Making the decision to go through the pain is a tough one and we will resist it for as long as we can. Over time; however, adversity will always strengthen and instill a greater awareness of the warrior spirit that resides inside each of us. I would encourage you to ponder which of the following applies to you.

Consider whether the reason you are doing whatever it is you are doing at this moment is because it's easy and the path of least resistance or because it's right and the path of most resistance. If it is not either of those then consider whether you are simply choosing to stay stuck. Self-knowledge of what is going on for you can create a shift and begin your flow.

These questions can extend far beyond grief and bereavement. They could be considered and applied to any aspect of our lives.

There are lots of what I call prescriptions and risks at play when determining our path to the new life and the new you. Prescriptions offered up by society and risks taken by us. I will expand on those in the following chapter.

> **"May you allow the destination of leader inspire you to step forward."**

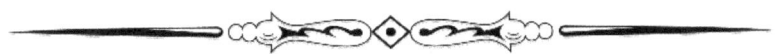

Chapter 29
"The Public Prescriptions"

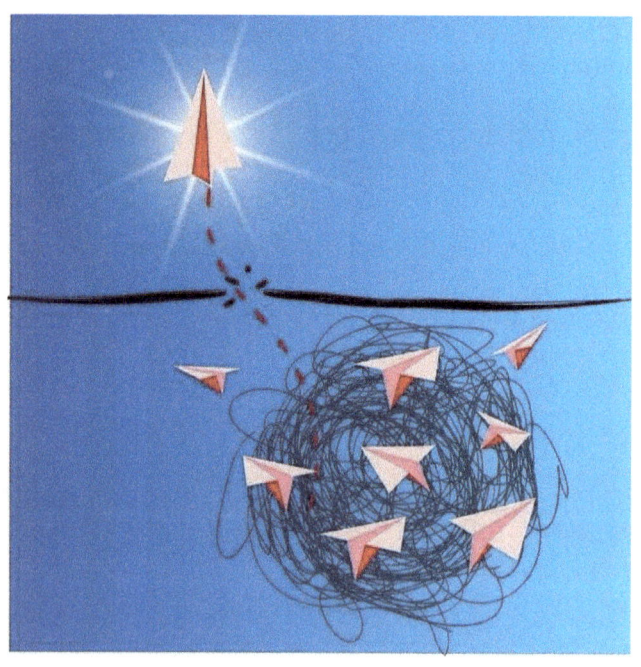

Destination Success

When bereaved folks are faced with the decision outlined in the previous chapter regarding engineering their grief path, the existence of a societal dichotomy shows itself. It is important to look at the opinions and options offered up to us by society and how we may view them.

Two very different schools of thought are perpetuated by society and often by those who have never been thrust into the role of bereaved parent. Society will impart the thoughts that we will never get over it or get over it. Our question and response to society would be well, which is it because you can't have it both ways.

When I would have someone express that Erin's death was something I may never get over, it immediately caused me to question and dispel any faith I may have held relative to my ability to work through the pain. It is critical for society to recognize that such expressions to us may very well conjure up such a result. Those expressions do not allow any consideration for joy or happiness restoration as goals or options. Society should also recognize that telling us to get over it will not be as easy for us as you think. Those snapshots of life called memories are a permanent fixture inside us. The good ones, the bad ones, and the ugly ones.

As bereaved parents we can't have it both ways so I guess it would be whichever one we choose to adopt. At least that is what society leads us to believe. The belief that either one is available. The problem is neither works if you are someone who is looking to restore happiness and joy in your life.

"A special message for Moms and Dads"

We will often take the direction of someone else only to discover doing so is not in our best interests. I would encourage you to

consider whether we might accept that direction because we have been subjected to perceptions by others of us being in a permanently dysfunctional state. The other scenario that may cause us to accept that direction is because we are made to believe we are not in a state that would have society see us as competent.

I was personally subjected to both those scenarios and I continue to trust strides are being made though they can often feel very slow to us coming to fruition

As well-intentioned as this direction from others may be, rest assured it can be detrimental and an impediment to our progress especially if that someone else has no experience as a bereaved parent. I wasted a lot of time giving credence and thought to what was shared with me by many people who really did not have any idea at all of what my world looked like. Such is the importance of the development of your own flow as discussed in the previous chapter.

When we experience a loss the normal responses are supposed to be just that. Whatever comes up for us are our struggles to be worked through. We are designed to have the ability to handle it; however, much time can pass before we recognize that possibility. It is not supposed to be hidden, masked, or diagnosed as something else. It often is though. Again let me point out there are exceptions here as well. There are always those with extenuating circumstances or lifestyles which could inhibit the healing process.

Apparently we are allowed to have dysfunctional families but the natural dysfunction that occurs after a tragedy can often be construed as a no-no. Though a temporary state for us, it is especially frowned upon by society and not accepted as I believe it should be, as it is supposed to be, and as it needs to be. Being either truly functional or truly dysfunctional only occurs when we are directing it. As in any situation in life, responsibility rests within and applies to all.

I am not an advocate of we must stay locked in the pain, we will never get over it, or get over it. I am an advocate of working to access all the potential you have inside you to get the job done; accompanied by as much understanding and non-judgmental support from others as possible.

Some think it is in God's hands. I believe in God and I believe he is there for us but he has no intention of doing the work for us. He will assist in getting us through by providing what we must be open to seeing and accepting. Those clues I call them which when embraced and put into the mix become valuable additions to guiding us along the way.

"May you allow the destination of success inspire you to step forward."

Chapter 30
"Risk and Reward"

Destination Survivor

It was not long after I had made my decision about which path I had chosen to travel to find my way back to the joy of life and stepped into it that the awareness of risks being taken by me and the rewards I was availing myself of came to the fore. It quickly became crystal clear to me that I would be required to exercise and exhibit a level of healthy courage. It was refreshing to see how that showed itself to me once I had decided to select a path set to my own standards and that would be travelled in my self appointed time and space.

When this important decision has been made with a clear mind, void of interference by those who have never lost a child including the experts, it is deserving of respect and acceptance by the outside world. When I experienced my enough is enough day and wanted to do my grief work, I chose the path described above and in doing so, integral parts to processing this component showed themselves while not devoid of setbacks along the way.

At the end of my journey, I clearly recall being able to honestly answer yes to all that I had experienced. This was a great journalling exercise and the visual was impactful. I highly recommend it.

My decision and journey yielded the following mix of risks and rewards.

Yes, I had lost friends.

Yes, I had family members distance themselves.

Yes, I had managed to work through the pain and succeeded in recreating my own self and life.

Yes, I had restored my happiness and joy of life.

Yes, I had endured being shunned and criticized.

Yes, I had survived becoming fodder for the gossip mill.

Yes, I had proudly exemplified grace under fire.

Most life decisions consist of risk and reward elements and how we choose to face our grief is no exception.

No one should be surprised by any of the foregoing. Any goal in life we set that others either do not agree with or are uncomfortable with is usually resisted, deflected, or rejected by them. It will be done with all kinds of reasons as to why we shouldn't choose this path when the response should simply be an agreement from others expressing "Well, okay then. I respect your decision and am here for you". What another beautiful gift that would be.

"A special message for Moms and Dads"

Trust yourself enough first and once you have completed your path, you will be able to build in others the trust in you that perhaps they lacked in the beginning.

When you enjoy a successful conclusion to your personal path decision, you will be so very grateful to you that you did. Having others believe in you is a wonderful thing but self-belief is the more powerful force and will get you to where you want to go.

Let your own self and others know that you are going to learn to get comfortable with being uncomfortable. That you shall be taking the time you need. That you will decide when you are tired enough of the pain. That in doing so you will achieve what others may call impossible. That you will restore your freedom from the binding chains of pain and recapture your joy of life. To thine own self be true and own that the reason it will all happen is because you are simply enough.

The animals of nature have great survivor instinct and use it without question or delay. Humans are part of the animal kingdom. We were born with survivor instinct also; yet, we are not nearly as proficient at stepping into survivor mode as the animals. We must develop the endurance and survival skills that will drive us to never give up.

You are smart enough, capable enough and deserving. You may not feel it, see it, or even believe it but your enough is intact. It does become clouded, hidden from view, injured, tormented, and buried underneath our deep, dark pain but is waiting to be released.

"May you allow the destination of survivor inspire you to step forward."

Chapter 31
"Grace Under Fire"

Destination Pride

Grace is a quality that is an illuminating performance in the grief process exhibited by bereaved Moms and Dads. In case you have not recognized it as such, let me say we are often clear examples of grace under fire so to speak.

When we speak of grace thoughts of a kindliness may come to mind. Grace can be a beauty of motion or action and represents love, mercy and compassion.

Those definitions are encompassing of our greatest need from others when we are feeling so devastated. Bereaved parents would greatly benefit from a level of leniency being extended by others when we are in that place of attempting to keep our heads above water. Interestingly enough the automatic manifestation of those definitions of grace happens for us because we have been so severely thrust into the awakening of life's fragility. At least that was my experience and what I have come to recognize and accept.

Through the years I have had many people share how much they have admired what they believed to be courage in my journey from sorrow to joy. I believe that was a partial misread and they were actually witnessing courageous grace, aka grace under fire. I never saw myself as courageous at all though certainly upon reflection, I came to realize how very critical rebuilding the courage had been during the journey. If anything, I felt like the exception to the rule as finding other bereaved parents who had been fortunate enough to work through their grief and return to joy was a minority number. Healing the loss of our loved one does not necessarily return us to the joy of life all on its own. Because our loss changes who we are fundamentally in such impactful ways, many of the components we are required to work through are issues somewhat removed from our loved one being gone. We must be accepting of the loss of our own self and the personal rebuild process shared in all of these chapters. My heartfelt wish is that more Moms and Dads are able to return to their joy of life. Our joy of life is a critical component in getting back to recapturing a sense of peace and

serenity to our lives. It is what is necessary in order for us to strike a balance that allows for making our loss somewhat palatable as missing our children is with us for ever.

"A special message for Moms and Dads"

To this day I continue to be intrigued by all I had to learn and revisit while working toward the completion of my grief journey. A journey which was many years in the making. Some of the qualities I have as a person and hold near and dear are ones I always had; others are ones I developed while on the journey. I just didn't know how important they were or how very capable they made me feel until my journey was done. They are priceless gifts and lessons I feel blessed by after having travelled and survived my path from sorrow to joy.

It is interesting that the behaviours we yearn to have extended to us while we are doing our grief work and are not always provided are the exact same ones we are perpetuating and it may very well be not recognized by us at the time.

I can tell you that when the work is done, you will have given yourself the opportunity and ability to reflect back and see that it was you, who, even under the most dire of circumstances, was the one who was the most accommodating with regard to bolstering those behaviours that define grace. Hold onto that thought and know it to be true.

Even if those behaviours describing grace were not part of who you were before your tragedy, they will be at the end. Tragedy has a way of accelerating the value we place on grace and all that it brings to self and others. We are gifted in a bittersweet way, with a true and clear picture of what mercy and compassion look like. They very much become an important part of the new you.

I would encourage all of you to recognize this aspect of your being, whether it has been forced upon you or not. To be a person of grace is not something everyone gets to experience and it is a quality deserving of high regard by others and our own self.

Death is a part of life. That is a reality. We should always respect the fact that one kind of loss is no easier or harder than another. They are simply divergent. The road map to restoring happiness has many routes to the common destination of pain free joy. We become the experts and a fine example of reaching out to others. Taking ownership of our quality of grace is an inspiration for self and others. Kindly feel free to join me as the perceived exception to the rule and together we can manifest the new norm.

"May you allow the destination of pride inspire you to step forward."

Chapter 32
"The Mask Parade"

Destination Vision

Welcome to a component of our grief journey that can find bereaved Moms and Dads sporting the unintentional and often unconscious to us mask. Participation in the mask parade is open to us and everyone else.

The mask phase is one we can participate in regardless of the type of loss. There doesn't even need to be a loss. The world is overrun with people who are living their lives masked. This is not exclusive to bereaved parents by any means although I do believe we stay in this phase longer than the average person.

The mask may be worn by the bereaved as long as there is a concern of being misunderstood, rejected, or talked about. It is easy to fall into the belief that wearing it will hide the pain but it never hides our pain. It only hides our fears. Some of us will wear the mask while conducting business and living life in the outside world. Then there are some who don't mind going out and letting the world see exactly what is going on.

Interestingly enough, what the world sees is never our true reality and we are only kidding ourselves if we believe the mask is hiding anything we are feeling. It is true the eyes are the window to the soul and bereaved or not, people see what they are ready, willing, and able to see. As mentioned in a previous chapter, what is going on is usually missed. Often making direct eye contact can be difficult for both sides.

"A special message for Moms and Dads"

Allow me to share some words to describe what is truly going on for us and what our eyes would reveal to others should they choose to look straight into them. The explanations above as to why we wear the mask are related to the following aspects of ourselves and our life that are temporarily disabling us.

Bearing in mind we may not even recognize and be able to explain to another what we feel, especially in those early days and weeks, we are experiencing anger and sadness, pain and isolation, shock and confusion, fears and tears.

All the while we may be exposed to the following words being used by others to describe us during interactions with them or by them to third parties. Others may see us as being cynical, stubborn, strong, bitter. Another misread.

We can be easily offended when those words are spoken to us. They are simply confirmation for us that others do not really understand. When others take a moment to put themselves in our shoes, they might have a slight chance of comprehending why we would be offended.

My personal story around being labelled goes like this. Erin passed in December and the following year one of my siblings was hosting a family dinner. I believe it was either on the Thanksgiving or Christmas of the year following Erin's accident.

At that point in time I was still very much reeling from our loss and unbeknownst to me was far away from being healed and returning to joy. I was unmoving in that place of trying to come to terms with the W5 of it all; that who, what, where, when, and why with so many questions remaining and yet to be reconciled. The circumstances around the dinner table provided what I felt was an opportunity to speak up about one of those burning questions; that being who was going to be accountable for her accident?

This sibling had no children yet felt she could respond by accusing me of being cynical and telling me I needed to get past all of that. I remember thinking to myself that perhaps she too would be cynical if she was ever a Mom and one of her children died. I didn't see what I was sharing as cynical at all. It felt more like frustration, sadness and anger to me; however, upon reflection I

believe even cynicism would be most appropriately acceptable under the circumstances I was finding myself facing. Whether it was cynicism or not, in that moment an awareness of the unenlightenment that existed for others came to the fore. Both intentional and unintentional ignorance can run rampant around us. For the most part, though, we would not respond to a label comment because we may not have the energy nor is it really our truth. It just seems that way. What needs to be shared is the truth which is we feel broken. Doing so would be simply uplifting to both sides. Unfortunately, in that moment for me, I had not yet arrived at being able to communicate that truth to others. May my sharing this experience provide an avenue for you to share openly your truth during those times of being labelled.

Just expressing how broken you may feel and that a hug would be great may elicit a response from others letting you know it is okay and that they are there for you. Take a moment and ponder how much energy both sides have just saved by doing so and at the same time been fortunate enough to experience something priceless. Truth happened, listening happened, and acceptance happened.

When we are willing to take our pride and ego out of the equation, we become the recipients of extraordinary ordinary miracles. Pride and ego in combination are always based in fear and we must become fearlessly passionate and passionately fearless. Fears of rejection, change, failure, acceptance, and success are all worthy of consideration. Any one or more of them will be applicable to any circumstances we may find ourselves in and finding difficult to move from.

"May you allow the destination of vision inspire you to step forward."

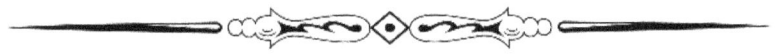

Chapter 33
"The Delicate Dilemma"

Destination Support

Welcome to yet another component of this piece meal grief journey which can find everyone at odds.

A wide and diverse assortment of holidays and special days to face and manage throughout a year exist for all of us. They include the birth and death days of our children, Valentine's Day, Thanksgiving, Halloween, Christmas, Father's Day, and Mother's Day, just to name a few. Then there are the celebratory special events that take place within families; birthdays, anniversaries, weddings, graduations, and back-to-school. Again, just to name a few.

In the years following our child's death, none of us approach these events any longer without feeling somewhat apprehensive. Everything worthy of consideration impacts everyone. Collectively thoughts of what to do and what not to do come to mind. We are faced with whether we change tradition or not. Are we even going to celebrate or not is a decision to be made; all the while contending with do we all agree or disagree?

Holidays are those times when discord can surface. Not only between the immediate family members of the child who has died but extended family members and friends as well. In efforts to simplify this complex aspect that surfaces upon the death of a child, please consider the following attitudes.

October 1st is often a date which brings to mind holidays which are fast approaching. I mention this date in particular for the benefit of everyone. It would not be uncommon for others to see a change in the demeanour of bereaved parents at this time of the year and we must all be very patient with each other as holidays and special events approach.

Compromise on the part of both sides is a key element to navigating and surviving the holidays. Agreeing to disagree is

okay and meeting in the middle is the way to go should you be wishing to not add to the discord.

For the outside world folks I would encourage you to ask for permission to give input to the bereaved during these times. Know that acceptance/rejection of the input request is not negotiable. We need you to embrace any change without judgment while respecting and honouring whatever it is we can manage. It is not a time for name calling or labelling. Respecting the memories that are no more and which play a huge role in the level of difficulty we experience during the holidays is appreciated.

For the bereaved I would encourage you to create only that which you can manage and feel up to celebrating. Put yourself first and follow your heart. Make a decision incorporating at least one piece from each person in the immediate family as to how the special day will be recognized. Make no more than a 20% change each year. By undertaking that 20% change per year concept, within five years the full cycle of change will have been completed.

"A special message for Moms and Dads"

For us, holidays and special events seem to have the power of evoking in us a barrage of feelings. They are often ones we don't want to bother with, depending upon where we are in our journey, how long since our loss, etc. Building an awareness of that for you and the outside world folks may illuminate what we may not be able to articulate. The holidays do not cause us any more grief. We are living the grief every day, holiday or not. However, they bring extras for us to cope with when the grief plate may already be overflowing.

For example, it may be very difficult for us to step into Thanksgiving. Thanksgiving is a time when, just as the name implies, we are to give thanks. When we are sad, angry, and

disillusioned, the only things we may feel we have to give thanks for are the hits we have been afforded. The last thing we may want to do is cook a celebratory dinner, set the table and find ourselves carrying that place setting we no longer need back to the cupboard. We don't want to not be able to buy the food items our child loved.

I clearly recall being there. I remember it being interpreted by others as my looking for attention or feeling sorry for myself. More misreads.

The following chapters will provide an expansion on particular holidays and special days that can be the most burdensome.

"May you allow the destination of support inspire you to step forward."

Chapter 34
"The Patchwork Holidays"

Destination Coping

Expanding on the topic of holidays and special events, this chapter is dedicated to sharing information meant to assist everyone in their navigation of those celebratory times that can create some of our biggest hurdles.

As a bereaved Mom, two of mine were Christmas and New Year's. The Christmas hurdle was expected; the New Year's one surprised me. I shall go out on a limb and presume that what I share could apply to most or all grieving Moms and Dads; regardless of what the season is referred to or how it is celebrated. I refer to the season as Christmas as that is what I celebrate and the only version I can speak to with any credibility. It is never my intention to offend or negate any culture and I respect the diversity of our current world.

My thoughts on Christmas before and after the death of my daughter were far removed from each other for many years.

"Christmas"

Before Erin passed I would have described Christmas as that magical season filled with dreams, wishes, hopes, ordinary miracles and the trust that it will all come true. It seems to be the only time of the year when everyone may feel it is socially acceptable to express love freely. It is obvious to all how warm and welcoming people are and how many are walking around smiling, saying hello, and exhibiting great patience in stores. This is all happening between people who do not even know each other. A time when strangers become our friends.

I have often given thought as to why we are able to do that. I wonder if it may be because the season has a way of creating a feeling of safety and comfort to do so. We feel it is okay, acceptable, and are allowed at this special time of year. Perhaps it is one of those ordinary miracles or simply our first Christmas gift.

Christmas has been a favourite of mine over the years. I was a Mom who always made Christmas a big deal for the family. Lots of secrets, the dinner, baking, decorations, making popcorn rope, shake and guess the gifts games, fun, loving and kind. I carried the traditions I had enjoyed as a child with me into my adult life and did my best to recreate the same for my own family.

It was the time of year new toys came into the house. None were purchased throughout the year except perhaps for a birthday and the girls were always excited and looked forward to Christmas with anticipation and joy. I never started to prepare for Christmas until around the middle of December. I would take a full day and do the shopping for everyone amid the hustle and bustle of busy stores. I loved doing that. Interestingly though, in 1984 I had purchased and wrapped everything in November and clearly recall sitting on the sofa one evening about a week before Erin was killed. Everyone else was in bed and asleep. There was a fire on in the woodstove and I wrote a letter to my Mom wanting her to know how very peaceful the house was and how at peace I was feeling having prepared for the holidays in such a different way that year. Little did I know how shattered that peace would become in such a short time.

After Erin passed all the above that I used to enjoy at Christmas became the stressors; even more than the absence of my sweet girl. Her absence was something I was doing my best to cope with and manage on a daily basis anyway. That was nothing new. The season that was magical to me and all that it brought became so burdensome upon the death of Erin, or so I believed. I used to think that but have come to learn that this, too, shall pass.

I did not love Christmas in 1984 when I missed out on all that love of strangers. The season held no appeal the year Erin was killed though it was celebrated in usual fashion for the sake of her almost 5 year old surviving sister. I really cannot tell you how I managed to get through that first Christmas. It remains a blur to this day and

I only have few and far between glimpses of it. We did celebrate though. After all, how do you not prepare a snack for Santa and not have him arrive for an almost 5 year old. The answer is, you don't not do it.

I would probably be safe in saying that I was feeling the same way as other bereaved Moms and Dads upon the approach of the season. The feeling of impending fear and dread; however, I have come to realize that my perception was not truly accurate. It was not the fear and dread or the season causing those feelings. It was the coping aspect.

As taxing as Christmas and special events through the year are for the bereaved; the sheer weight of it does not exclude anyone and both sides get to carry it until such time as we compromise and meet in the middle as shared in the previous chapter.

Anyone who has not experienced our loss would not be aware and therefore not be sensitive to the challenges presented and the necessary changes either. Becoming familiar with all of this aids in having the communication breakdown which can be so prevalent on these occasions become somewhat less conflicting and create more clarity.

"A special message for Moms and Dads"

Coping for the bereaved parent, no matter what time of year, is an additional daily chore and more often than not, a minute by minute one. We work at coping with life. Christmas and all holidays or family celebrations are magnifiers to us and simply put more on our plate at a time in our lives when the plate is already overflowing and full of confusion that our new reality has given us.

We can often be heard expressing that we are not going to celebrate. We may not be up to it and often cannot imagine celebrating

without our loved one. These are normal and expected views and no one should be shocked by them. We already know that the moment our child died, we were no longer who we once were. We no longer have the life we once had and to have an expectation of the Christmas we once enjoyed is unrealistic. Grief and loss cause our priorities to get rearranged and the level of importance we used to place on them does also. That is okay. It is part of this piece meal process. As especially difficult as that first Christmas was for me and for many years after, it did, over time, return to one of celebration. Hold on to that thought for you.

"New Year's"

After a brief reprieve from Christmas ideas for the New Year get underway. A time for parties, socializing, and plans for implementing new wants and needs are being given consideration. A time of fun, joy, and looking forward to embracing the new. We are busy with decisions we are making willingly. At least that is how it was approached by me for many years before Erin's passing.

As a bereaved Mom that first holiday season I believed once I had mastered and survived Christmas, I would be able to breathe a sigh of relief. I hoped it would be smoother sailing for a bit only to discover the New Year's celebration was approaching and as it did, the perceived calmer waters I was counting on became rougher all of a sudden. They began to churn and made me feel as though I was drowning.

I have a couple of thoughts around why that might be the case. Our unconscious is an interesting facet of the human brain and we could easily liken it to an iceberg. When we look at an iceberg, we are only visually exposed to 10% of it. The remaining 90% is underwater. Just close your eyes for a second and imagine the magnitude of that amazing miracle. Brain activity works in much the same way in that it is estimated only 5% of it is conscious. The remaining 95% takes place unconsciously and not only do we have no real control over it, we are also not even aware that it is taking place. That 95% applies to our habits, emotions, beliefs, values and so much more.

On a conscious level when we are confronted with one of those unexpected waves, whether during holidays or not, they can hit us like a ton of bricks. Bear in mind it has usually been conjured up from that unconscious place. Once we recognize them from whence they come, it allows us to stop questioning self and stop being hard on self knowing they are not anything we have control over. The gift we are being provided is a clue that something needs attention though we may not recognize it as a gift at the time.

"A special message for Moms and Dads"

When I was exposed to my first New Year's without Erin, it became a piece of my letting go process which none of us get to avoid. A piece we often attempt to delay because it is so very painful. As much as we want some things behind us, we don't want to let them go. It is a catch-22.

Having to let go of the year our child died is akin to another loss on top of the original event. We can become fearful about the fading of things we will always want to recall in the future. Yes, things do fade but as I have mentioned before, it is temporary.

Unlike decisions we made willingly before our loss, those same decisions can often feel forced upon us after our loss. Resolutions, for example. Those promises we used to make to self that often never came to fruition. Most people approach January 1st with prospective resolutions in mind; however, we can often be found approaching it with mixed feelings and swirling emotions. Those resolutions that perhaps we used to make can now appear mundane and unimportant to us in the big picture.

I made the decision to no longer make traditional resolutions. I moved from there to a place of I will aim to and am sharing that idea with you; trusting it may help you transition from one year to the next. A great benefit of I will aim to is it is available to you on any day of the year. It is not specific to New Year's and you get to begin whenever you choose. It is also not specific to only the bereaved. I believe it would be safe to say that through the years all of us have struggled with those resolutions. Deciding to move from resolutions to aims can apply and be beneficial to all.

My initial list was comprised of what I believed I could manage at that point in time. I would revamp and update it as I travelled along, based on how I was doing. My list looked like this and it is my hope it may provide you with some triggers to get you started.

I will aim to smile at least once a day.

I will aim to get out of bed at least once a day.

I will aim to inhale at least 5 minutes of fresh air once a day.

I will aim to stand alone.

I will aim to speak my truth to self and others.

I will aim to have it not matter if others disagree.

I will aim to take ownership of all inside me that I have to work with.

I would encourage everyone to create their own I will aim to list. May it reflect all that you are going to do for yourself over the coming days ahead of you that will move you forward. A list that can be updated as many times as you want. A list that forces you

to access and use those intangible internal elements we all possess. Your persistence, your love, your intelligence, your inner strength just to name a few. The more you use them, the stronger you will become. Doing so will bring you brighter days and nights.

"May you allow the destination of coping inspire you to step forward."

Chapter 35
"The Birth Day"

Destination Warmth

This chapter's information is for everyone to absorb as we continue to have a look at getting past celebratory events. I would be remiss in not spending some time on the day our child came into our lives as it has the power to bring a host of feelings to the fore. For some it is the biological day of birth; for others it may be the day you adopted your little one. No matter the circumstance that placed them in our care, the details never fade. It is a day of remembrance always for everyone who knew our loved one.

My sweet girl began her earthly life story on Saturday, June 3, 1978, at 8:08 PM when I delivered her into the world. She arrived blessed with beautiful blue eyes and blonde hair. To this day I can clearly recall that special moment when that little soul with whom I had already developed a bond all those past months was given life by me. That moment of rebirth from inside Mom is a moment never forgotten and stays with us for ever and always. The next defining moment happens when our precious gift is ready to be placed on our chest and the recognition for us of how very fragile and dependent they are on us shows itself.

After Erin passed, June 3rd was one of my toughest days and remained so for many years. For a long time I felt burdened as it approached. It had a way of conjuring up reminders of what we were now being robbed of seeing or experiencing ever again because doing so was so very painful for a long time.

Having you successfully undertake an evolution from the difficult *birthday* to the heartwarming *birth day* perspective is my wish for the bereaved and everyone else. Whether you choose to do so or not is up to you and I trust you will do what you feel is best and works for you.

"A special message for Moms and Dads"

Please ponder the following. When the anniversary date of your loved one's death arrives, do you relive every moment of it?

I believe it would be safe to say a lot of us have that experience and it can be many years before we are able to take charge of this component of our journey. Let me, with the highest degree of respect and for the purpose of this message, call this day by its true name. The "death day". In sharing that, it brings to mind the following to consider.

When the anniversary date of your loved one's birth arrives, do you relive every moment of it?

If you are able to do so without any pain, that is great. If it is too difficult or hurtful for you I encourage the following.

Changing our perspective from painfully acknowledging the *birthday* to reminiscing about the *birth day* can make a world of difference. Was it not a day of joy, happy tears, love, and happiness? Allow those warm memories to wrap themselves around you on your loved one's special day and be open to sharing them with others. Again, when the time is right for you. Sharing gives others the opportunity to do some healing and also provides them with unspoken permission to talk about our child; something we love and often feel doesn't happen often enough.

We should always remember, too, that for some, the birth day and death day are one and the same and our hearts ache for those parents.

As previously mentioned, just as on the day our child passes we are thrust into new and foreign territory, so are we on the day they came to us. We have added another dimension to self in both instances.

Reflect back on your dear one's birth day story and allow the fond remembrances support you in moving forward. I strongly

encourage you to journal the story as doing so is a good first step to being able to share it verbally later on.

Include as many details as you wish. All that you remember. Not just the birth but the visitors, the gifts, the going home. The overall beauty of everything was a gift and a miracle. This wonderful dedication and celebration of the one who left you too soon will bring a smile to everyone's face. It may only be for a minute for some; however, it will help to lessen the dread we can all experience as the day approaches.

Embrace the date from the perspective of the birth day as opposed to the birthday and it may just become more comfortable for you and everyone else. Doing so opens the door for others to share their memories they have of time spent with your loved one.

"May you allow the destination of warmth inspire you to step forward."

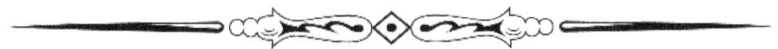

Chapter 36
"The Exceptional Legacy"

Destination Gratefulness

This chapter is meant to bring to light two aspects of our journey that perhaps not all of us experienced yet a large percentage have. Aspects that may very well be kept private or secret by grieving Moms and Dads.

"Yes, I Knew"

We could call this first aspect yes, I knew. Yes, I knew refers to a view the bereaved are reluctant to share for fear of negative feedback or caustic remarks from others. Others tend to hold the opinion it is not really anything we truly experienced or felt. They believe it is something we come up with after the death as a coping mechanism of sorts.

Not true. However, let's allow the cat out of the bag, shall we? I think we should because it is an important piece of our grief journey puzzle which can provide a little peace and comfort to us and others when revealed. I know I am not alone with what I will share. I have shared this view with thousands of bereaved parents in efforts to determine I wasn't the only one. I discovered two things. There are many who are of the same view and experience and there are many who were happy and relieved to have it out in the open. I was years being able to articulate my yes, I knew.

From the day Erin was born, I knew I would never see her grow up and that she was a gift on loan to me for as long as the good Lord was going to deem necessary and I clearly remember expressing those words to a very dear friend at the time of her birth. I didn't have anything that could back those words up except a gut instinct. I didn't even know where the thought came from.

Later in Erin's life, when I would ask her what she was going to be when she grew up, she would just look at me, shrug her shoulders and tell me that we didn't have to think about that. I never had with her the experience of a nurse today, a hairdresser tomorrow as is so typical of children her age. Oh, how I would

push away that thought of knowing she wasn't here for long when she would say those things. In the same way I pushed that thought away at the time of her birth. It was always almost as though she somehow knew she was not going to be here long; however, not recognizing it for what it was on a conscious level.

The bereaved love when this truth for us is not only revealed but respected, accepted and not questioned as well. I would urge others to give some thought to any interactions you had with our loved one. Chances are you may have had similar experiences and like us did not want to give it any credence at the time as it can be scary and not anything anyone wants to face. Should that experience be one you had, sharing it with bereaved Moms and Dads would be so comforting to those who feel the same. Simply ask us if we ever felt we were not going to have our child for long to jump start this conversation.

"A special message for Moms and Dads"

May the personal experience I shared above resonate with you. If it has then I know you understand, you get it and not find it odd at all.

There are lots of instances when either we the parents, the child, or both are suspect of the impending event. I believe that those children who have passed before their parents, for the most part, live more life experiences than the average person their age. They seem to cram more in, learn more, teach more, and are usually wise beyond their years. They are often peacemakers by nature and have an almost translucent quality about them in photographs.

Should you be a yes, I knew Mom or Dad, acknowledge you are not the only one and sharing it does assist in moving forward. It matters not what others think. Those who had the pleasure of

meeting our special one should know everything we want to share about them.

"Gift of Life"

We shall call this second aspect their gift of life. This is a part of our journey that immediately presents itself in association to the death of our loved one. An aspect that may or may not typically be shared by us but a decision many of us face.

More often than not one of the biggest doses of reality in our situation is being queried at the time of our child's death about whether or not our child is an organ/tissue donor. I know it was for me. When that was posed, my world turned upside down because it was being asked immediately following doctor's confirmation that our little one had not survived. They have been pronounced dead and we are reeling from that news and then bombarded with this loaded question as donations are very time sensitive.

My immediate and personal response without giving it a second thought was that yes, we would donate whatever we could. Then information is shared about what is viable and what isn't. When I was informed only her corneas were viable, that opened a floodgate of tears for me along with wanting to know why that was the case; only to be informed everything else was too damaged. Remember, I did not know what had happened exactly, only that her school bus was involved.

The decision around donations brings the nightmare we are sitting in to a conscious level like nothing else. Should you be someone who knows bereaved parents who have made this bittersweet decision, be sure to validate it. We are asked to make this choice when we are at our worst and still manage to make it happen.

"A special message for Moms and Dads"

If you have had an experience similar to mine, kindly recognize the depth of such an encounter and pat yourself on the back for coping and managing such a task. By acknowledging that feat and recalling it on those many days ahead of you when you feel you are not going to make it through, be reminded of how you were able to navigate, decide, and execute those decisions around donations at a time when you were so devastated. That reminder will serve you well in moving forward.

Donations are gifts that come from tragedy. We are provided the opportunity for our dear one to give the gift of life or the gift of improved life to another. It becomes part of their legacy for us and a blessing to their recipient.

"May you allow the destination of gratefulness inspire you to step forward."

Chapter 37
"The Faith Angle"

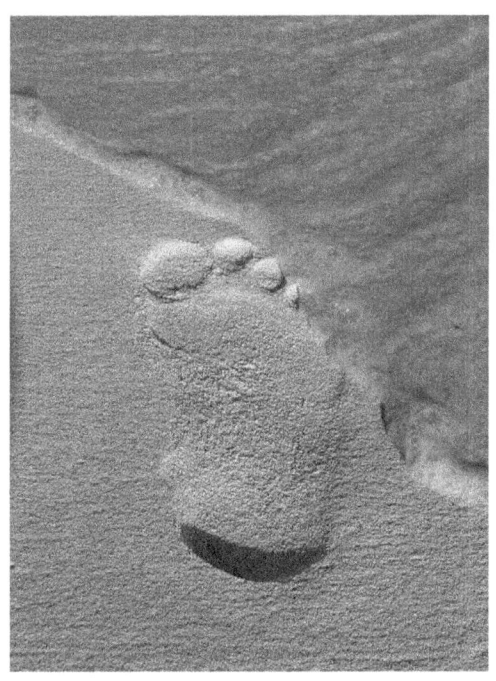

Destination Reality

The ripple effect felt upon the death of a child is not only far reaching but diversified as well. It could be likened to a variegated flower. One that is the same colour but consisting of many shades reflecting the fluctuating depths of the pain being experienced by each individual.

Everyone is impacted; from those associated with the bereaved on a small scale to the largest of scales when there are many lives lost of people with whom we had no association. All hearts are affected and why wouldn't they be; grief and sadness are heart issues.

This chapter will provide a snapshot of how the faith angle of our grief can provide an opportunity to be shared in a manner by all clergy that would be truthful and beneficial to all. We will look at who is impacted by the faith aspect in our lives and recognize that how ingrained it is can elicit a wide range of opinions. As with politics, agreeing to disagree would not be surprising with this topic and is okay.

Let me paint a picture relative to the funeral event from my perspective as a bereaved Mom in those early days. The church is filled with an assortment of individuals who come from all areas of our life. They mourn for us, they mourn with us; all the while, perhaps, not feeling as comfortably adequate as they would like.

I have no regrets around the life I had with my little girl; however, to go back and redo the funeral, not that I would want to, is something that would have been handled differently. Only in having travelled the grief path I have completed did I reach the conclusion I am going to share.

"A special message for Moms and Dads"

There are always great messages delivered from the pulpit and faith perspective which I believe to be important; however, connected to that for some bereaved parents is the truth that our faith may be quite difficult to hang on to in those early days. We can find ourselves questioning our faith. For others, their faith becomes their sustenance.

When I reflect back on my Erin's funeral event I find myself thinking that the following words by the clergy would have been my preference. I did not realize it at the time though.

"Your faith may be lost, **temporarily.**"

"You will experience anger, **temporarily.**"

"You will experience shock, **temporarily.**"

"You are in a dark and shrouded place, **temporarily.**"

"Such is the state of your new normal, **temporarily.**"

"It is all okay. It is to be expected."

Articulating the above in that church would have been what the bereaved family would connect with and be comforted by in the knowledge that all is not permanent. It would have also provided information to everyone attending and build an awareness for them and a sensitivity to our existing reality.

There may be some who hold the opinion that the above would be too much information, too soon. However, it would take care of a challenge a lot of bereaved parents face and that is one of too little information, too late.

The coping with the life changing event thrust upon us begins the moment our child has died and the above, in my opinion, simply provides validation to our state of being. Confirmation that we are experiencing natural responses. Sharing this information with our clergy may very well aid them in easing pressure perhaps felt by them when having to deliver a funeral service relative to the death of a child.

"May you allow the destination of reality inspire you to step forward."

Chapter 38
"Right and Wrong"

Destination Warrior

Welcome to an overview of two more components of our grief journey that can cause much distress. I am referring to accountability and justice. Both are essential aspects deserving of respect. The level of accountability and justice a person, bereaved or not, searches or yearns for is directly measurable to the circumstances being faced and they can be wide and diverse. Seeking accountability and justice in the beginning for bereaved Moms and Dads may appear to others as though we are looking to play the blame game; however, it is really about moral rightness, in my humble opinion.

Eventually everyone will come to realize that these aspects, when resolved to what we can live with, will bring peace and provide another move towards joy; however, usually not recognized until we are at the end of our journey.

"Accountability"

The dictionary will tell us that accountability means being answerable to a particular action or being in a position of liability. Those meanings imply it would take work to get accountability. Work takes effort and effort takes energy and time.

In taking a moment to reflect on just how accountability is doing in the world, I have come to the conclusion that it is almost extinct and an endangered moral principle. The lack of it reaches far beyond the scenario of a bereaved family and extends into many other areas of life as well. It can be lacking in the workplace, in organizations and institutions, in government, in families, between individuals, and anywhere else that may come to mind for you. I have come to learn accountability will only exist in the world when we are no longer willing to walk away without it.

The lack of accountability may be the result of another moral principle I see at risk in today's world. The one called integrity. My personal definition of integrity is saying what you mean, meaning what you say and having no excuses. It could also be referred to as follow up or follow through.

I believe accountability is directly related to integrity and hold that opinion as it has been my experience on more than one occasion. Where there is no accountability, there is no integrity and where integrity resides, accountability is a non-issue.

"A special message for Moms and Dads"

Make yourself aware of all I have shared above before deciding to step into the accountability arena. My experience has shown me it can take years for accountability and justice to surface and still may not yield the desired outcome.

I invested over ten years with no one taking responsibility for my daughter's death to this day. The accountability journey could be its own book. I was able to reconcile this when I came to realize that I had not failed in my efforts to seek accountability and justice. The system failed me. That recognition enabled me to simply shift everything to where it belonged and take ownership of my efforts which moved me to being able to let it go.

"Justice"

The dictionary will show us justice means to act or treat fairly, to administer deserving punishment or reward, and fair mindedness. Another aspect that implies the same level of time and energy investments as is applicable to accountability.

In the circumstances of some bereaved parents, justice becomes part of their journey. We need and want to know what happened to

our children. It is one of the most important and painful elements of our grief journey and requires respect and support from others, not questions.

Whether justice prevails or not, it is our core value system that is impacted and in a very emotional way. Should you be a person of principle and who lives life taking responsibility for what you say and do, then you no doubt have the same expectation of others and will always do your best to command it of them. That is a right and privilege that comes with being a person of integrity in my mind.

"A special message for Moms and Dads"

In my circumstance I was looking for justice based in moral rightness. We can be very adamant about justice and accountability and it is our right and privilege to seek outcomes we can accept. Our loved ones were priceless and after a tragedy the value we placed one them immediately switches to the responsible party. Transitioning to that goes against everything we are, know and live.

Our beliefs, morals, ethics, and principles are what is challenged when justice just is or is not. When we are forced to go against our natural flow that resides inside us and drives us; it is chaotic, conflicting, and oh so overwhelming. Achieving no justice is a huge barrier to moving forward and we will fight to the end. Moral rightness should always prevail, but sadly, does not.

My personal experience in these arenas recommend you heal from the loss of your special one first before attacking accountability and justice. It will take time for the restoration of your strength and courage which you will need to fight these battles.

"May you allow the destination of warrior inspire you to step forward."

Chapter 39
"The Arrogant Airs"

Destination Guide

Welcome to the behaviour that can often be extended to us as we attempt to seek the accountability and justice alluded to in the previous chapter. The behaviour is called patronization and I feel quite confident in believing I am not alone in having experienced it from others in my role as a bereaved Mom.

Patronization can take on more than one form. It can be an act of being gracious to another, giving support or it can be the adopting of an air of condescension toward others.

Apparently it can be a good thing when utilized in the vein of being gracious or supportive to another; however, it is important to look at it in the context of those times when another behaves in an offensively condescending manner toward us. There are times when its nature is one that is being directed for the purposes of making us feel incompetent or stupid; or at its worst, being looked down upon or frowned upon.

It could be we don't even consciously recognize those behaviours from others as an act of patronization; however, that is what it is.

Bereaved parents seeking to understand the circumstances of their loved one's death are a good example of those who can be treated with patronization. It is delivered to us by those who are not ready, willing, or able to own up to any role they may have perpetrated in the death of our child or the events surrounding same.

There are many forms of patronization and reading on will expose you to some of them that bereaved parents often have conveyed to them in their efforts to glean accountability and justice.

"A special message for Moms and Dads"

It can be quite disheartening for us when on the road to seeking accountability and justice to experience patronization. I was

exposed to blatant patronization for a decade from those for whom I had questions while attempting to get clarification about what happened to my daughter. Patronizing behaviours can include but are not limited to being told to get over it, you need therapy, or having someone agree with you just to get rid of you.

Such examples are a reflection of others wanting to opt for the easiest and least time consuming path for them and all are signs of disrespect. I would encourage you to consider who may be treating you in a patronizing manner. You may even have to make a list to remember them all.

Once you have the responsible parties identified, you may choose to shift gears as it relates to any circumstances involving your being the recipient of such. You can do so simply by changing your response to the other person. They may not even recognize their behaviour as a patronizing one and it may just be our individual job to inform them of such and nip it in the bud, so to speak.

I always strived to do so with grace, dignity, and diplomacy of course. It is not my wish to add any credence to what they are telling me I need to be and do. I usually handle it by letting them know the following. Feel free to adopt any or all of it. Select whatever fits your circumstance.

"I strongly believe no one person is inferior or superior to another."

"We are all created equal."

"Everyone deserves respect and honesty."

"What you are saying makes me feel snubbed."

"Allow me to build an awareness for you."

"Be aware and sensitive to the fact that your advice or opinions can be received as patronizing in nature even if well intentioned."

"You may wish to change your approach in how you communicate to me as doing so may allow you to do the same for others in the future."

"Now, shall we try again?"

Patronization is a component of our journey that we often have to take in hand and convey to others that it does not work for us and will do nothing to provide the answers we are looking to receive. Often, too, we have to remind others that were we not ready for the answers, we would not be asking the questions.

"May you allow the destination of guide inspire you to step forward."

Chapter 40
"For Ever More"

Destination Hope

Welcome to a topic that I trust will be beneficial to all, grievers and non-grievers. That is my wish for you.

Everything in life has a beginning and an ending. That not only applies to people and relationships of all kinds; it also applies to the animals, the plants, jobs, homes, social events and so on. The list is as long as our circle of life which encapsulates a complete journey of phases and stages. Young, old, or anyone in between can be exposed to one of life's firsts at any point in time. We really don't control anything other than self.

Nevertheless, the word forever is one that is spoken and heard many times throughout our lives. We say the word and use it in a way that denotes no ending. How many times have we or someone else said I will love you forever, you will forever be in my prayers, and maybe we will be best friends forever. As beautiful as that is, the truth is no one can guarantee forever and nothing in life is forever.

Just as a circle is comprised of 360 degrees, I liken our circle of life to having the same. When we are able to look upon it that way, we open the door to navigate whatever we are facing in 360 different ways simply by moving that one little degree to gain a new perspective. When one approach does not work, we have 359 others to choose from. The destination never changes, only the route and we often have to change it more than once to reach the befitting conclusion. This is a concept we could apply to each component of our grief journey if we wanted and is one that could be applied to any area of a person's life, bereaved or not.

Let's assume someone might be struggling with this word forever while working through their grief or life issue. I will share how changing perspective just that one degree can be a step forward. From this point on, I will be using for ever as two words, not one.

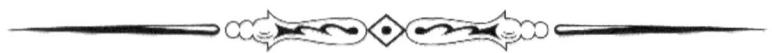

Imagine using for ever as two words and giving consideration to having it mean for as long as it is supposed to last. Think about that for a moment. Upon reflection you may come to realize that is what we actually experience in life. Our for ever with anyone or anything is just that.

"A special message for Moms and Dads"

For ever is not in our hands and we, the bereaved folks of the world, know that to be true better than most. There is no doubt we would all say our children were not with us for as long as we would have liked or wanted. Perhaps, though, they were with us for as long as it was supposed to last.

It is interesting that at the end of The Lord's Prayer it states "the power and glory for ever and ever, Amen." Always two words. That makes me wonder whether it was ever meant to become one word. Perhaps when it did, our perception of its meaning changed. Something to consider.

If what I have shared here is what you happen to agree with or can come to agree with, then there is comfort in the knowledge that our children were with us for ever in a physical way.

Our heart connection, spirit, soul; whichever speaks to you, cannot be broken or interrupted. Our loved ones are with us always and for ever more. The cord is never severed and the joy they brought to us in life they left behind for us to recapture.

As always, I can only share what worked for me in the trust it may help you. You get to select the pieces that resonate with you and I appreciate your being open. I do know shared information can often make the difference in living sorrow or joy.

"May you allow the destination of hope inspire you to step forward."

Epilogue

"Reclaiming the joy of life for a bereaved parent is a painfully difficult and lengthy journey. Once completed though, it is a declaration of who you are. You will have, as some may say, achieved the impossible. Be very proud."

After giving much thought to what would be my closing comments to Our Compatible Grief, I am going to share a very personal undertaking that I was able to complete free of pain and tears.

It is a letter I wrote to my dear Erin many, many years after her death. I had finally completed my grief journey, was back to experiencing the joy of life and it was an easy thing for me to do. May you enjoy it.

When you are able to talk about your child, write about them, share whatever you want about them to others without becoming emotional or shedding tears you can take that as a sign that you are doing okay. A sign that you are at or near the completion of your healing and close to joy, once again. All the while still missing them each and every day, minus the pain.

I would encourage you to write your special one a letter when you are ready. It is a beautiful gift to them, for you and anyone you wish to share it with. A piece to put in place until we meet our babies again, and we shall.

Much love,

Deborah

"My Loaned Child"

Dear Erin,

I am writing a letter to you which is going to be part of a collection of letters to daughters from their Moms in a book being published by a friend. A letter to you, my sweet girl, to share what you have only been able to experience, from a distance. Yet, it is a certainty in your Mama's heart that you have been part of it all along and will be for ever and always.

Being my first baby, you were my big test at being a Mom and a parent. I had stepped into a world I did not know with much excitement and joy, while also feeling scared about everything that would require of me. I had fears of bathing you properly, feeding you, nurturing, guiding, and loving you. It did not take long, though, to realize it was not a job of the brain, it was one of instinct and the heart.

You, my first child, arrived at my side at 8:08 PM on Saturday, June 3, 1978. A beautiful blonde-haired, blue-eyed girl weighing in at 7 lbs 8 ozs and who loved to snuggle from the get-go.

Then at 2:11 PM on Thursday, December 6, 1984 you left your Mama's side through no fault of your own and I was devastated.

Looking back, I have come to learn that the day you left this earth ignited those same feelings I had the day you were born.

I had been forced to, once again, step into a brand new world and life. Not with any excitement or joy this time but with pure fear and sadness. I had to learn to let you go, continue

my life without you physically by my side and recreate myself and my life. I did not know how to do that. It was not anything I had been prepared for or ever could have been. I ended up realizing the same thing as when you were born though. This journey of pain and hurt I was thrown into was not a brain job either. It, too, was one of instinct and heart.

There was a time so very long ago that lasted many years when I could never see me living a life of joy without you. I did not believe I would ever have happiness again. However, over much time and work, I came to realize that the joy you brought me when we were together was a gift you left me upon your departure. It did not go with you. It was and remains one of my greatest gifts from you. Just as you were and still are for me, my darling girl. You have been one of my greatest achievements and I want you to know I have come to also learn that your birth, life, and death were designed to serve the purpose of have your Mama discover her own life's purpose.

Did I ever tell you that I knew you were a gift loaned to me as soon as I saw you in that first moment in time when you were at my side? I can remember clearly a good friend coming to visit us in the hospital shortly after your birth. She looked at you, looked at me and said "She is so beautiful, Debbie, beautiful Little Miss Erin"; to which your Mama immediately said "She is a gift from God, for me to have for as long as he feels is necessary."

As our time together passed, over the six short years we were together, you and I had many times where that thought I had rang so true. Do you remember when I would ask you what you were going to be when you grew up? You would always

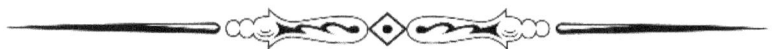

shrug your little shoulders, look up at me, smile and answer me with something like "You know, Mommy, we don't have to think about that". That would scare me so much but I would not let you see how scared I was. I just kept pushing those thoughts I had of not ever going to be able to see you grow up away and kept on embracing, enjoying, and cherishing every moment we had and when everything ended on that cold December day, I was and still am so very glad we had done so.

I still miss you, my dancing and singing partner. We had so much fun together! You were always ahead of your time. Loving, kind, very much a free spirit and a peacemaker by nature. I want you to know that even though you were only six years old when your job was done, the life you had was crammed with so much more than is usual for that age. You taught me so very much. I just wish you hadn't finished your job here as quickly as you did.

Your leaving started my devastation and you returning to me some years later with a clear and concise message redirected my painful journey onto a path that eventually brought me to my destination of joy and happiness, once again. The message that came to me out of the blue; the one and only time I have heard your voice since your leaving as I have never dreamed of you. The miraculous message that was and remains to this day to be a huge gift you have afforded your Mama, even in your absence, which is really what made it so powerful. The message that you did not feel any pain when your accident happened. It was a comfort for me to learn that directly from you as I had always been so discomforted by the thoughts of what you perhaps felt that day at a time when we were not together. A time when I had no opportunity to do

that thing we both loved so very much; when your Mama would hold you, hug you, and reassure you that everything would be okay and that you were safe in my arms.

I want you to know I have felt your presence many times since we've been parted. I know when you are here. I know you are, every day, still by my side as we reach out to lots of other people from around the world who have also had to be separated from their babies far too early. Your contribution to the world lives on and will continue to do so, even after we are together again.

We will meet again. I know you are as certain of that as I am and we will pick up our singing, our dancing, our hugs, and our loving each other at where we left off and it will feel as though this space that is now between us never existed. I know you are waiting for me and that brings me to another one of the greatest gifts you have given your Mama. You have made dying easy for me.

You are loved, missed, cherished, and treasured ~ for ever and always ~ and I have loved writing this letter to you, my sweet one.

Love always ~ Mommy ~ xoxo

THE END

www.ingramcontent.com/pod-product-compliance
Lightning Source LLC
Chambersburg PA
CBHW061229070526
44584CB00030B/4051